BOX FURNITURE

The Nursery

TOY CUPBOARD
WALL BRACKET   CHILD'S BEDSTEAD
CHILD'S WASHSTAND AND DRESSER
CHILD'S CLOTHES-PRESS   NURSERY CLOCK
CHILD'S CHAIR
CHILD'S BED-STEPS   CHILD'S STOOL
OCTAGON NURSERY TABLE

Color Scheme:
　White,
　Blue.

Woodwork:
　White paint.

Furniture:
　White, with motif taken from curtains and stenciled in blue.

Walls:
　Four-foot dado of blue with white above, motif stenciled in blue.

Ceiling:
　White.

Curtains and Bed-covers:
　White muslin, or gingham with simple design in blue.

Play Aprons and Dresses:
　White, or same shade of blue.

Floor:
　Light wood in its natural state and shellacked. Blue rugs.

Plants:
　Growing plants with white blossoms and forget-me-nots.

BOX FURNITURE

HOW TO MAKE A HUNDRED USEFUL ARTICLES FOR THE HOME

BY
LOUISE BRIGHAM

ILLUSTRATIONS BY
EDWARD H. ASCHERMAN
FROM DESIGNS BY THE AUTHOR

Fredonia Books
Amsterdam, The Netherlands

Box Furniture:
How to Make a Hundred Useful Articles for
the Home

by
Louise Brigham

ISBN: 1-4101-0170-3

Copyright © 2003 by Fredonia Books

Reprinted from the 1910 edition

Fredonia Books
Amsterdam, The Netherlands
http://www.fredoniabooks.com

All rights reserved, including the right to reproduce this book, or portions thereof, in any form.

In order to make original editions of historical works available to scholars at an economical price, this facsimile of the original edition of 1910 is reproduced from the best available copy and has been digitally enhanced to improve legibility, but the text remains unaltered to retain historical authenticity.

DEDICATED TO

CYNTHIA P. LANE

THE GOOD ANGEL OF MY CHILDHOOD WHO BY HER NOBLE EXAMPLE OF UNSELFISH LOVE TO A MOTHERLESS CHILD WAS THE FIRST TO SHOW ME THE JOY OF SERVICE; AND TO

JACOB A. RIIS

WHOSE BOOK "HOW THE OTHER HALF LIVE" INFLUENCED ME IN LATER YEARS TO LEND A HAND TO THE FRIENDLESS

FOREWORD

Among the many friends in Europe and America to whom my thoughts turn in grateful memory for their generous encouragement, I mention for especial thanks Mr. and Mrs. William D. Munroe, whose charming hospitality in the Far North made many of these experiments possible; Herr Professor Josef Hoffmann, of Die K. K. Kunstgewerbe Schule, in Vienna; Miss Virginia E. Graeff, for valuable help and suggestions; and to all "The Givers of the Tool Chest"

CONTENTS

CHAPTER		PAGE
	Introductory Chapter	3
I	The box in its simplest form	9
II	The box kept in its original form, with the addition of false bases and corner trims	23
III	The same principles as Chapter II, with the addition of circular cuts	39
IV	The box taken partially apart so that it loses its original shape	55
V	Combinations of Chapter IV	67
VI	Larger boxes, applying the same or similar principles as in Chapter V	87
VII	The box turned upon its side, with the cover and sometimes the sides removed	107
VIII	One or more boxes supported one above the other by either corner trim or legs	133
IX	Three or more boxes used in simple combination	155
X	The box taken partly or entirely apart and the material used in construction	177
XI	More elaborate combinations of the articles in the previous chapters and with larger and a greater number of boxes	211
XII	The same principles as Chapter XI, with the addition of framework	247

LIST OF INTERIORS

		PAGE
Nursery		*Frontispiece*
"Den"	I	10
Living-room	II	24
Twin-bed Room	III	40
College Boy's Corner	IV	56
Kitchen	V	68
Office	VI	88
Boy's Room	VII	108
School-room	VIII	134
Bedroom	IX	156
Studio	X	178
Invalid's Room	XI	212
Dining-room	XII	248
Club-room	XIII	294
Library or Study	XIV	296

LIST OF SUBJECTS

NUMBER	PAGE
1 Plant-box, 2	13
2 Child's Bed-steps, 1	14
3 Cast Pedestal, 1	16
4 Vine Vase, 2	18
5 Cane and Golf-stick Stand, 1	19
6 Vine or Branch Pedestal, 3	21
7 Miniature Plant-box, 1	27
8 Jardinière, 2	28
9 Scrap-basket, 1	30
10 Scrap-box, 1	32
11 Kitchen Stool, 1	33
12 Hanging Flower-box, 2	34
13 Perforated Scrap-box, 1	36
14 Hanging Lantern, 1	37
15 Footstool, 1. Child's Stool. Club-room Stool	43
16 Coal- or Paper-box, 2	45
17 Blacking-box, 1	47
18 Oblong Clock Case, 1	49
19 Upright Clock Case, 1	51
20 Nursery Clock Case, 1	53
21 Small Wall Rack, 2	59
22 Wall Bracket, 2	61
23 Vase Wall Bracket, 1	63
24 Kitchen Spice-box, 1	64
25 Pipe Rack, 1	65
26 Housewife's Handy Rack No. 1, 2	66
27 Kitchen Comfort, 2	71
28 Double Wall Rack, 1	72
29 Large Wall Book Rack, 1. Broom Shelf	73
30 Wall Book and Knickknack Bracket, 2	75
31 Housewife's Handy Rack No. 2, 2	78

NUMBER	PAGE
32 Magazine Rack, 1	80
33 Shoe Cupboard, 2	82
34 Housewife's Handy Rack No 3, 2	84
35 Flower-stand, 1	91
36 Soiled-linen Receiver, 1	93
37 Shirt-waist Closet, 2	95
38 "Notionette," 2	97
39 Office Washstand, 2	99
40 Desk Chair, 2	101
41 Quadruple Writing-desk, 1	103
42 Fireplace Bookcase, 2	112
43 Simple Bookcase, 2	114
44 Music-stand, 1	116
45 Office File, 1	118
46 500-volume Bookcase, 1	120
47 Bookcase with Drawers, 1	123
48 Boy's Book- and Game-table, 1	125
49 Wall Desk, 1	127
50 Bookcase Desk, 2	129
51 Odds-and-ends Stand, 1	137
52 Rolling Soiled-dish Stand, 2. Smoker's Table	138
53 Flower- and Book-stand, 2	140
54 Bedside Stand, 1	142
55 "Silverette," 1	144
56 Game-table, 3. Toy Cupboard	146
57 Twin-bed Night Table, 2	149
58 Nature-study Stand, 1	151
59 Photographic-material Stand, 2	159
60 Reference Stand, 1	161
61 Child's Clothes-press, 1	163
62 Umbrella- and Overshoe-stand, 1	166
63 Chafing-dish Table, 2	168
64 Washstand, 2	171
65 Octagon Nursery Table, 2	174
66 Kettle- and Cover-holder, 1	182
67 Nest of Benches for Kindergarten and Settlement, 1	184
68 Table Bookstand, 2	186

NUMBER	PAGE
69 Firewood or Newspaper Rack, 1	188
70 Dressing-table Chair, 1. Baby's High Chair. Child's Chair	190
71 Flag Wall Rack, 2	192
72 Picture Frame No. 1, 1	195
73 Mirror Frame, 1	197
74 Picture Frame No. 2, 1	198
75 "Dresserette," 2	199
76 Greek-cross Tea-table, 2	202
77 Child's Bedstead, 1	205
78 Invalid's Bed-table, 1	207
79 Teacher's Desk, 1	216
80 Boy's Work-table, 1. Kitchen Table	219
81 Window-seat, 2	221
82 Bedroom Window-seat, 2	224
83 College Corner Seat, 2	228
84 Single Wardrobe, 1	230
85 Double Wardrobe, 1	233
86 Spitzbergen Sideboard, 2	234
87 Allendale Sideboard, 2	238
88 Copenhagen Sideboard, 2	242
89 Corner Washstand, 1	252
90 Combination Washstand and Wardrobe, 1	255
91 "Shavingette," 2	256
92 Triple-mirror Dressing-table, 3	259
93 Dressing-table, 2	262
94 Washstand and Dresser, 2	265
95 Child's Washstand and Dresser, 1	269
96 China Closet, 1	272
97 Hall Stand, 2	276
98 Boy's Delight, 1	280
99 Club-room Corner Seat, 2	282
100 Combination Desk, Reading-table, and Bookcase, 2	289

ALPHABETICAL INDEX

	PAGE
Allendale Sideboard	238
Baby's High Chair	190
Bedroom Window-seat	224
Bedside Stand	142
Blacking-box	47
Bookcase Desk	129
Bookcase with Drawers	123
Boy's Book- and Game-table	125
Boy's Delight	280
Boy's Work-table	219
Broom Shelf	74
Cane and Golf-stick Stand	19
Cast Pedestal	16
Chafing-dish Table	168
Child's Bedstead	205
Child's Bed-steps	14
Child's Chair	190
Child's Clothes-press	163
Child's Stool	44
Child's Washstand and Dresser	269
China Closet	272
Club-room Corner Seat	282
Club-room Stool	44
Coal- or Paper-box	45
College Corner Seat	228
Combination Desk, Reading-table, and Bookcase	289
Combination Washstand and Wardrobe	255
Copenhagen Sideboard	242
Corner Washstand	252
Desk Chair	101
Double Wall Rack	72
Double Wardrobe	233
"Dresserette"	199
Dressing-table	262
Dressing-table Chair	190

	PAGE
Fireplace Bookcase	112
Firewood or Newspaper Rack	188
500-volume Bookcase	120
Flag Wall Rack	192
Flower- and Book-stand	140
Flower-stand	91
Footstool	43
Game-table	146
Greek-cross Tea-table	202
Hall Stand	276
Hanging Flower-box	34
Hanging Lantern	37
Housewife's Handy Rack No. 1	66
Housewife's Handy Rack No. 2	78
Housewife's Handy Rack No. 3	84
Invalid's Bed-table	207
Jardinière	28
Kettle- and Cover-holder	182
Kitchen Comfort	71
Kitchen Spice-box	64
Kitchen Stool	33
Kitchen Table	219
Large Wall Book Rack	73
Magazine Rack	80
Miniature Plant-box	27
Mirror Frame	197
Music-stand	116
Nature-study Stand	151
Nest of Benches for Kindergarten and Settlement	184
Newspaper Rack	188
"Notionette"	97
Nursery Clock Case	53
Oblong Clock Case	49
Octagon Nursery Table	174
Odds-and-ends Stand	137
Office File	118
Office Washstand	99

	PAGE
Perforated Scrap-box	36
Photographic-Material Stand	159
Picture Frame No. 1	195
Picture Frame No. 2	198
Pipe Rack	65
Plant-box	13
Quadruple Writing-desk	103
Reference Stand	161
Rolling Soiled-dish Stand	138
Scrap-basket	30
Scrap-box	32
"Shavingette"	256
Shirt-waist Closet	95
Shoe Cupboard	82
"Silverette"	144
Simple Bookcase	114
Single Wardrobe	230
Small Wall Rack	59
Smoker's Table	139
Soiled-linen Receiver	93
Spitzbergen Sideboard	234
Table Bookstand	186
Teacher's Desk	216
Toy Cupboard	148
Triple-mirror Dressing-table	259
Twin-bed Night Table	149
Umbrella- and Overshoe-stand	166
Upright Clock Case	51
Vase Wall Bracket	63
Vine or Branch Pedestal	21
Vine Vase	18
Wall Book and Knickknack Bracket	75
Wall Bracket	61
Wall Desk	127
Washstand	171
Washstand and Dresser	265
Window-seat	221

PREFACE

Two summers on the island of Spitzbergen taught me, more than all previous experiments, the latent possibilities of a box.

Our camp was located seven hundred miles north of the Arctic Circle; Hammerfest, Norway, five hundred and thirty-five miles to the southeast, was the nearest point from which supplies could be obtained. Ice and snow cut off the settlement from the outside world for eight months of the year. The provisions and other equipment necessary for the camp of eighty miners and workmen had to be carried in boxes on the ships that came from the mainland during the four summer months. When the portable house which was to be the home of the manager, his wife, and myself as their guest, had been put up and the supplies unpacked, the boxes began to accumulate.

Here was an opportunity for putting to a practical test previous experiments in the making of "box furniture." I asked my host to give me the privilege of showing how these "odds and ends," usually considered worthless, could be utilized in making attractive furnishings for a comfortable home. No lumber was available in Spitzbergen, for, though we found during the short summer a beautiful arctic flora and "famine bread" (the edible moss often used by explorers), the "polar willow," growing but two inches in height, was our only tree.

Cut off from other materials, the possibilities of the box seemed greater than ever, and the work, which daily grew in interest, was commenced. As I worked in that far-off marvelous land of continuous day, surrounded by mountains and glaciers, I felt anew the truth, so familiar to all, that work to be of real value must be honest, useful, and beautiful, and Ruskin and Morris spoke as clearly in the arctic regions as in the settlements or studio in New York.

A pleasing incident of that summer occurred when we welcomed some members of the Walter Wellman exploring expedition who came to pay us a visit. One of the explorers, noting our comfortable little cottage with its attractive box furniture, turned to my hostess and said: "You have the northernmost civilized home in the world, for though our camp is one hundred miles nearer the pole, yet we have no woman there to grace it, and without her there can be no home." In many other homes the box has been found most useful, and its great value as an educational force I wish here to note.

The Prince of Monaco, who visited our arctic home, seemed as much pleased as the Danish peasant who watched by the work-bench. Among the most enthusiastic admirers to be found of "the possibilities of a box" are the bishop, the mayor, the bank president, the capitalist, and the professor, while the elevator boy, the scrubwoman, and the working man have shown equal enthusiasm.

One feature that gave constant stimulus to the work was the friendly interest shown by people of different conditions and nationalities.

In the teaching of manual training the carefully prepared material given to the children often has a tendency to make them rely too much on externals. If the pupils could be encouraged to supplement their school work with materials found in the home, they would find near at hand a practical opportunity for creative activity and the working out of educational principles. What better opportunity for such uses can be furnished than by the box as found in or near every household? Here is an often neglected opportunity for the transformation of humble and despised material into objects of beauty and usefulness for the home.

Besides the educational and artistic values found in such work, there is also a wide economic significance in the use of the box. It is said that an American household throws away after one meal sufficient food to provide three meals for a French peasant family.

Boxes cost almost nothing, and so serve a valuable end as illustrative material for school and other experiments.

Though the economic value of the box and its especial adaptability for school and social work have been mentioned, experiment has proved that it can be used with artistic effect in the homes of wealth and culture.

The ideas in this little book have either been presented in theory or illustrated by practice in Spitzbergen, England, Norway, Sweden, Holland, and Germany, in the Social Settlement of Copenhagen, Denmark, in the Sunshine Cottages (the model homes where I lived in the foreign districts of Cleveland), in the studio as well as a working man's flat in New York, in the Elizabeth Peabody House, Boston, a vacation home for girls in Connecticut, and in the Bradley Republic "Allendale," near Chicago, as well as in a five-room apartment (my own home) which is being furnished as this book goes to the press. This is an apartment in a tenement on the East Side of New York City, with the typical kitchen, dining-room, two bedrooms, and a living-room, the second bedroom being used as a studio where furniture and curtains are actually created on the work-bench and loom at small cost, showing how the needs of a home may be practically and artistically met at a minimum expense through the utilization of the cast-off.

The suggestions here given are not only applicable for the uses already noted, but box furniture finds its happiest expression where limitations of space have to be considered. So the hall bedroom, the camp, the winter dwelling, the summer cottage, the steamer, the city office, the kindergarten and school-room, and even the foreign mission can be fitted up admirably in this way, and the furniture in each instance can be mated to the waiting space with a minimum of expense. As its practical value has been proved in both the Old and the New World alike, it is with the hope that the suggestions offered may be utilized by other workers in the home, be it rich or poor. To all who care for simplicity and thrift, utility and beauty, I send my message.

BOX FURNITURE

BOX FURNITURE

INTRODUCTORY CHAPTER

A WORD BEFORE BEGINNING

To avoid repetition in the descriptions, directions applying in common to all the various articles are here given, together with a few brief hints to help make the way smooth.

SELECTION OF THE BOX

The appearance of the completed articles made from the various boxes called for in this book will depend very much upon one's ability to obtain boxes that are in good condition. Therefore, select the best, discarding those that are out of shape and have serious blemishes, such as brands burned on their surface, knotholes, or other serious defects which will be difficult to obliterate. Many boxes are now made having "dovetailed" corners. If a side or an end is to be removed, this kind of box must be rejected.

SIZE OF THE BOX

The size given in the requirements is the actual *outside* dimensions of the box named. A box of equal size under another name (and there are many, as boxes of every imaginable size and shape are made) will generally do quite as well, and in many instances boxes not the exact size specified, but nearly so, can be used. The size called for, however, is *about* the size necessary to obtain the proper proportion of the article to be made.

DISJOINTING THE BOX

When the box is to be partially or entirely taken apart, first remove the cover, then loosen the joints slightly by gently tapping on the inside close to the joint to be severed until the nails are "started." Then tap the side or bottom (as the case may be), and from the outside withdraw the nail with the hammer claw. The box will readily come apart if both the cover and the bottom are removed.

It is sometimes necessary to take the box entirely apart, and plane its sections in order to remove serious blemishes and enhance its appearance, and put it together again. If the box is to be used with the side or end removed, it is better to withdraw too many rather than too few nails. Then close up and re-nail the joints and fasten the cover on again.

CORNER TRIM AND LEGS

The method of making the corner trim and legs is the same for all the articles. They are always made of a narrow and a wider strip nailed together to form a right angle (regardless of their length, although size of material called for varies), each side of the angle measuring alike. In joining them together, use small nails or large brads $1\frac{1}{2}$ inches long, driven about 4 inches apart.

NAILING

When nailing together the various parts, it is well to drive the nails so that their points will remain hidden. In joining boxes, the nails are driven from the inside of one box through its side, end, or bottom (as the case may be), into and through the abutting portion of the adjoining box. Use nails of the right length to project $\frac{1}{8}$ of an inch or more inside of the latter box, where the points should be bent over at a right angle, which is termed "clinching the nail." The size of the nails for the various pieces and the distance apart they should be spaced must be a matter of individual judgment of the worker; generally speaking, however, a nail having a length equal to the combined thickness of the parts to be joined is sufficient, unless allowance is to be made for clinching. Use brads when possible, or wire nails with small heads, and with a nail-set and hammer drive their heads slightly below the surface in order that they may show very little or be entirely hidden.

FINISHING TOUCHES

Select good covers for the doors or lids, and smooth the edges and surfaces of each article by planing, scraping, and sandpapering. All objectionable nail-holes near the edges and any similar defects may be filled with a mixture of putty and sawdust or pegs of wood driven in and trimmed off even with the surface. Pure putty will not absorb stain, therefore add as much sawdust as the putty will hold.

Spools sawed in half and screwed on make very good home-made knobs. Serviceable buttons for the doors can be easily made of wood if desired. The prepared paints and varnishes sold in most of the paint-stores make an excellent finish. Flat stains of the dark hues are also very good, but the light ones are too transparent and will not cover well.

DECORATION

The simple motifs shown in the several interiors are an adaptation of the "Hoffmann method" of utilizing the square as the basic principle in decoration. They are shown in combinations of two or more squares, or parts of the same, as in the Nursery Interior. This method makes it possible to have attractive rooms decorated in a simple manner without any especial art training. It may be so applied that nail-heads and other imperfections will be less conspicuous, as shown in the Kitchen Interior. It may also be effectively woven into rugs, appliquéd or stenciled on the table-covers and hangings, and stenciled on the side walls.

TOOLS

The hammer is the most useful of all the tools required, therefore get a good one, a carpenter's claw-hammer, selecting one with a claw that will draw nails that project but slightly above the surface. The tools necessary to make the simple articles are named first, and others may be added from time to time, as the opportunity offers:

- 1 Three-foot Folding Rule
- 1 Adz-eye Claw-hammer, 16 oz. (Hammond's No. 3)
- 1 Cross-cut Saw, 20 in.
- 1 Rip-saw, 20 in.
- 1 Stanley Iron Block Plane, No. 9½
- 1 Brad-hammer, 4 oz.
- 1 Drawing-knife, 8 in. blade
- 1 Hardened-blade Try-square, 10 in.
- 2 Firmer-chisels, ⅜ in. and ¾ in. (Buck Bros.' No. 2)
- 2 Firmer gouges, ¼ in. and ½ in.
- 1 Sloyd Knife, No. 7
- 1 Brace, 8 in. (Barber's No. 223)
- 3 Auger-bits, ½ in., ¾ in., and 1 in. (Russell Jennings')
- 1 Iron Pad Keyhole-saw, No. 2
- 1 Pair Winged Dividers, 6 in.
- 1 Handled Brad-awl, 1½ in.
- 1 Round Knurled Nail-set, $\tfrac{1}{8}$ in. cap
- 1 Stanley Iron Smooth Plane, No. 3
- 1 Round Hickory Mallet, No. 4
- 1 India Oil-stone, No. 29, in Iron Box
- 2 Screw-drivers, 3 in. and 8 in.
- 1 Beech Miter-box, 18 in. long

NOTE. As boxes of the same make and kind vary slightly in size, and as boxes other than those specified, but of nearly the same size, may be selected, it is deemed wiser to make no attempt to state in figures absolute dimensions for the material (other than the boxes called for) under the head of requirements for each illustration.

CHAPTER I

THE BOX IN ITS SIMPLEST FORM

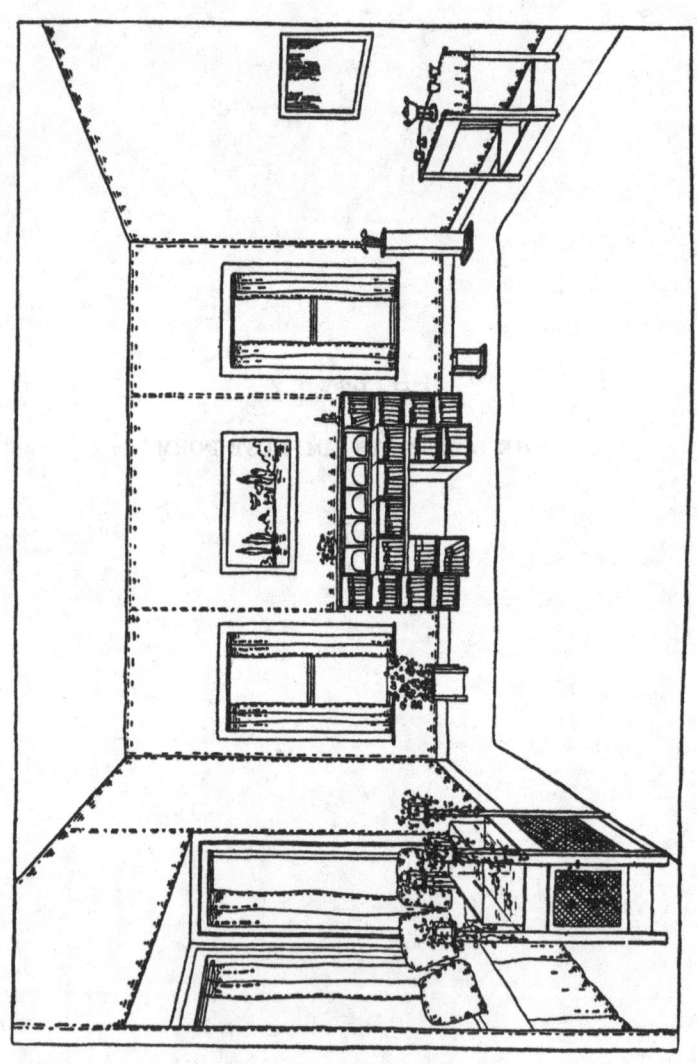

The "Den"

NATURE-STUDY STAND   JARDINIÈRE
FIREPLACE BOOKCASE   SCRAP-BOX
CANE AND GOLF-STICK STAND
SMOKER'S TABLE

Color Scheme:
> Dark mahogany (deep red).
> Light buff.

Woodwork:
> Dark mahogany.

Furniture:
> Dark mahogany.

Walls:
> Light buff, with motif stenciled in same color as furniture.

Ceiling:
> Buff in lighter tone than the walls.

Hangings, Pillows, and Window-seat Cover:
> Homespun in natural linen color, with motif stenciled in mahogany tones.

Curtains:
> Deep cream fish-net, with motif woven or embroidered in heavy floss of mahogany colors.

Floor:
> Painted same color as furniture, with jute rugs of natural color, and mahogany shades in the border.

Plants:
> Growing plants or cut flowers with yellow, orange, or red blossoms.

CHAPTER I

Illustration 1

PLANT-BOX

Box with cover removed, otherwise left intact.

Illustration 2

CHILD'S BED-STEPS

Three boxes placed top side up; two have covers removed and hinged as lids, otherwise left intact.

Illustration 3

CAST PEDESTAL

Box placed on end, otherwise left intact. False bottom and false top added.

Illustration 4

VINE VASE

Box placed on end; cover removed, otherwise left intact. False base added.

Illustration 5

CANE AND GOLF-STICK STAND

Box placed on end; top end removed, otherwise left intact. Facing strips and two false bases added.

Illustration 6

VINE OR BRANCH PEDESTAL

Box placed on end; top end removed and used as shelf, otherwise left intact. False base and facing strips added.

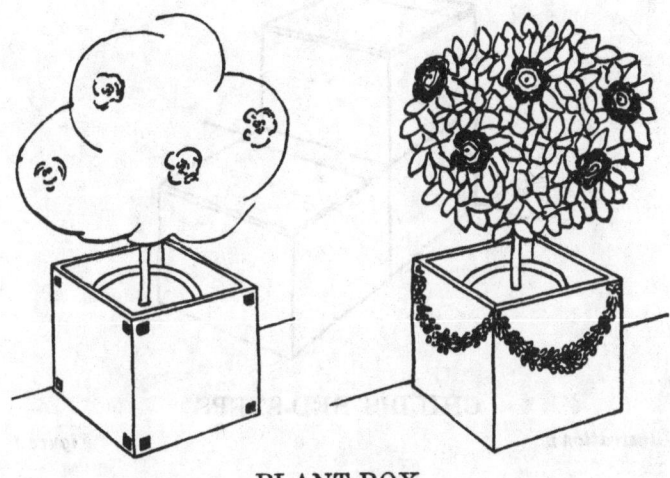

PLANT-BOX

Illustration 1 *Figures 1 and 2*

Requirements:
Body. 1 Bottled-bean Box (about 7¾ in. deep, 11¾ in. wide, 12¼ in. long).

Construction:
Remove the cover carefully from the box and fill all nail-holes or other imperfections with putty or wooden pegs, and stain or paint. When thoroughly dry, a design or motif may be painted or stenciled in oil color on the sides.

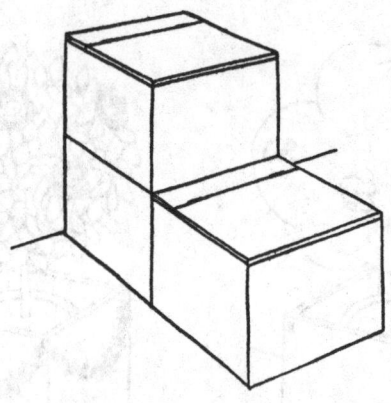

CHILD'S BED-STEPS

Illustration 2 *Figure 1*

Requirements:

Body. 3 Canned-fruit Boxes (about 10 in. deep, 9 in. wide, 14 in. long).

Hardware. 4 1½ in. brass butts and screws.

Construction:

Remove the covers from two of the boxes. Saw a strip 2 inches wide, the length of the cover, from each cover. Set these strips or portions of covers in their original positions on the tops of the boxes and nail them. Hang the balance of each cover to these strips with 1½ inch butts, laying them flat on the top face or placing them in the joint between the cover and the strip, if you prefer, and place the butts about 2 inches from each end of the box.

BOX FURNITURE

Nail the cover tightly on the third box and place it on the floor, top side up. Set one of the other boxes upon it with its cover side up and nail them together. Turn them on their sides and place the other hinged-cover box upon the side of the third box, or the box from which the cover was not removed, and nail them together. Turn them flat side down on the floor and they will be ready to use as steps and for holding shoes and stockings.

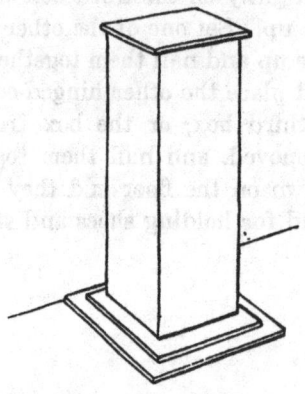

CAST PEDESTAL

Illustration 3 *Figure 1*

Requirements:
  Body. 1 Silk Box (about 7 in. square, 35 in. long).
  Top.   1 Piece ¾ in. thick, square 2 in. greater than the box.
  Base. 1 Piece ¾ in. thick, square 2½ in. greater than the box.
           1 Piece ¾ in. thick, square 4 in. greater than the box.

Construction:
Place the box on end with the bottom end up. Set the 2½ inch greater square upon it, allowing its edges to project evenly all around, and nail in place. Upon this square set the larger square, allowing it to project evenly, and nail it to the smaller square. This forms the base for the pedestal. Turn it upside down and stand it upon the base, then set the top on and nail it, allowing it to project evenly all around.

NOTE. As it may be difficult to obtain a silk box in some remote places, the body of a box without ends can be made from part of a packing box that is 35 inches or more long, by making four pieces ½ inch thick, 6½ inches wide, and 35 inches long. Put the body pieces together in such a way that one edge of each side will butt against and the other edge will lap over its adjoining side, thus:

BOX FURNITURE

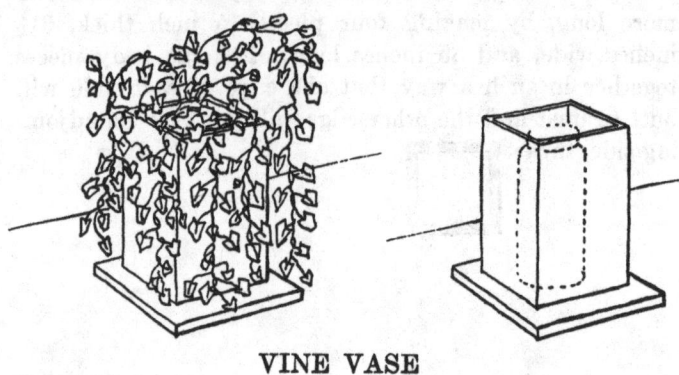

VINE VASE

Illustration 4 — *Figures 1 and 2*

Requirements:
Body. 1 Bottle Box (about 4 in. square, 8 in. long).
Base. 1 Piece ¾ in. thick, square 3 in. greater than box.

Construction:
Remove the cover. Turn the box bottom up and set and nail the base upon it, allowing the edges of the base to project 1½ inches on all sides.

NOTE. This Vine Vase is extremely attractive when used collectively, as shown in the Dining-room Interior, where five are in the window.

BOX FURNITURE 19

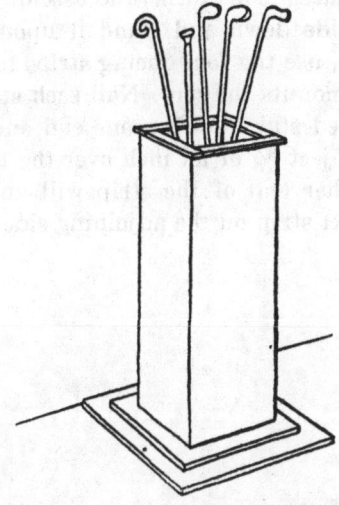

CANE AND GOLF-STICK STAND

Illustration 5   *Figure 1*

Requirements:

Body. 1 Silk Box (about 7 in. square, 35 in. long).

Base. 1 Piece ¾ in. thick, square 2½ in. greater than the box.
       1 Piece ¾ in. thick, square 4 in. greater than the box.

Facing Strips. 4 Strips ½ in. thick, 1¼ in. wide, and length equal to the side of the square of the box.

Construction:

Remove the cover or top end. Place the box on end with the bottom end up. Set the 2½ inch greater square piece upon it, allowing its edges to project evenly all around, and nail in place. Upon this square set the larger square, allowing it to project evenly, and nail it to the smaller square. This forms the base of the pedestal. Turn it upside down and stand it upon the base. For the top finish, use the four facing strips to form the square which surmounts the top. Nail each strip on the top edge of the pedestal, allowing one end and one side of the strip to project ⅝ of an inch over the face of the pedestal. The other end of the strip will butt against the side of the next strip on the adjoining side.

BOX FURNITURE 21

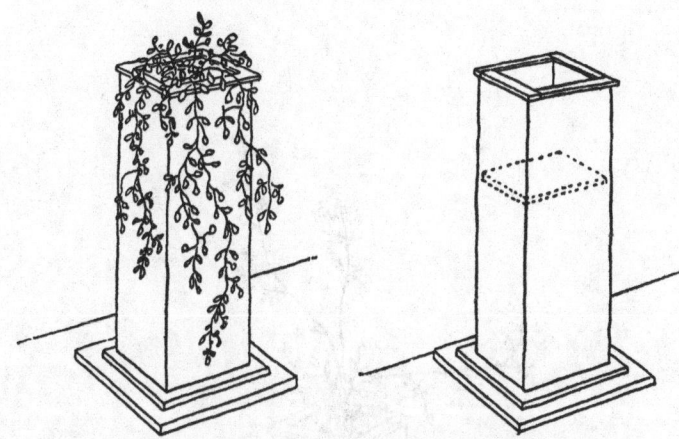

VINE OR BRANCH PEDESTAL

Illustration 6   *Figures 1, 2, and 3*

Requirements:

The same as for the Cane and Golf-stick Stand, Illustration No. 5, with the following addition:

Shelf. 1 Piece ½ in. thick, width and length to fit inside size of the box.

Construction:

The same as for Illustration No. 5. Then place the shelf inside the pedestal, 8 inches from the top end, and nail through into its edges from the outside with 1¼ inch brads.

BOX FURNITURE

22

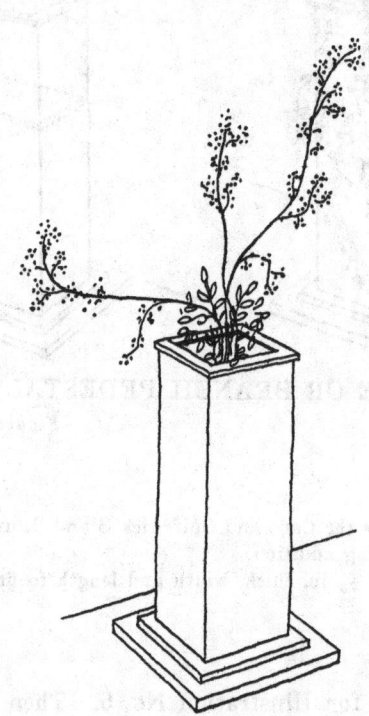

CHAPTER II

THE BOX KEPT IN ITS ORIGINAL FORM WITH THE ADDITION OF FALSE BASES AND CORNER TRIMS

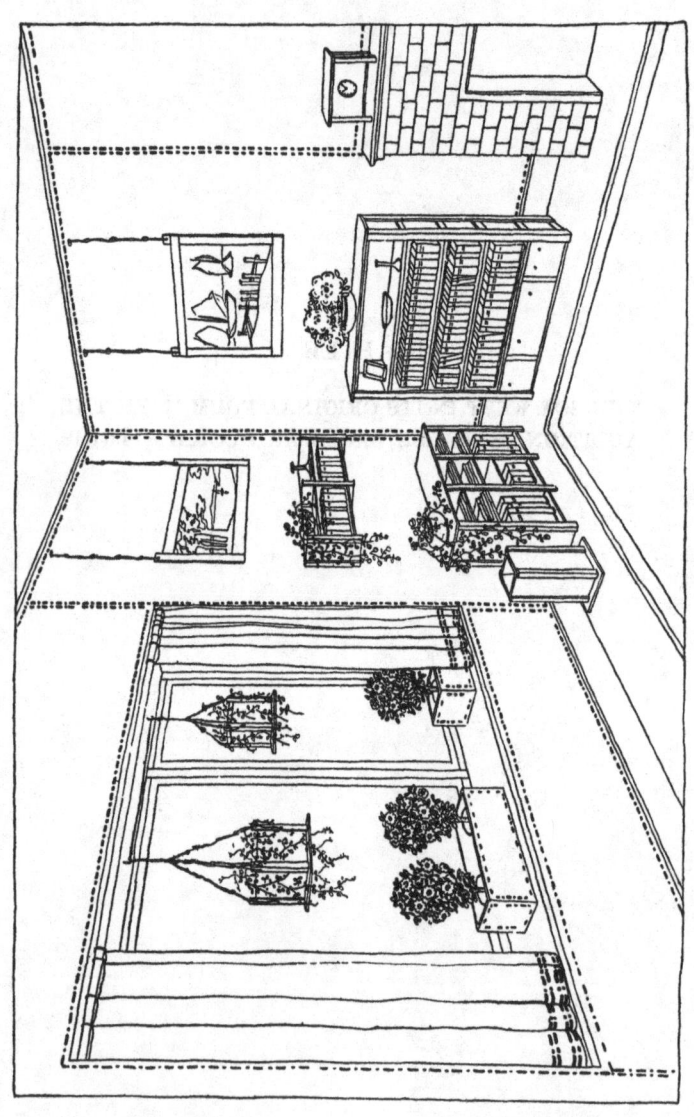

The Living Room

HANGING FLOWER-BOXES   PLANT-BOX
DOUBLE WALL RACK
MAGAZINE RACK   PICTURE FRAME NO. 1
BOOKCASE WITH DRAWERS
SCRAP-BASKET   OBLONG CLOCK CASE

Color Scheme:
    Black.
    White.
    Crimson.

Woodwork:
    Black paint.

Furniture:
    Black paint.

Walls:
    White, with motif stenciled in black.

Ceiling:
    White.

Hangings and Chair Pillows:
    Canvas in rich *crimson* (*not deep red*).

Curtains:
    White muslin, with motif embroidered in black.

Floor:
    Painted black, with rugs of crimson tones.

Plants:
    Vines, cut flowers, and growing plants with crimson or white blossoms.

CHAPTER II

Illustration 7

MINIATURE PLANT-BOX

Box placed top side up; cover removed, otherwise left intact. Legs added.

Illustration 8

JARDINIÈRE

Box placed top side up; cover removed, otherwise left intact. Legs and facing strips added.

Illustration 9

SCRAP-BASKET

Box placed top side up; cover removed, otherwise left intact. Corner trim and false base added.

Illustration 10

SCRAP-BOX

Box placed top side up; cover removed, otherwise left intact. Projecting corner trim and false base added.

Illustration 11

KITCHEN STOOL

A larger and deeper Scrap-box turned upside down.

Illustration 12

HANGING FLOWER-BOX

The Scrap-box with the addition of holes in the projecting corner trims.

Illustration 13

PERFORATED SCRAP-BOX

The Scrap-box with the addition of holes in each side.

Illustration 14

HANGING LANTERN

A larger Perforated Scrap-box turned upside down, with cover left on and one side removed and hinged as a door.

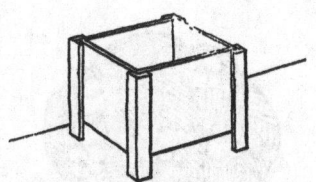

MINIATURE PLANT-BOX

Illustration 7   *Figure 1*

Requirements:

Body. 1 Salt Box (about 4 in. deep, 4 in. square).

Legs. 4 Strips ¼ in. thick, ¾ in. wide, 1¼ in. longer than height of the box. 4 Strips ¼ in. thick, 1 in. wide, 1¼ in. longer than height of the box.

Construction:

Trim off the three sides at the top of the box which contain the grooves that hold the cover. The top of the box will then be level or even on all sides.

Make the legs 1¼ inches longer than the height of the box after it has been trimmed.

Place and secure a leg at each corner, keeping the top of each leg even with the top of the box. Use wire nails 1 inch long. Sandpaper and fill imperfections with putty, and stain or paint any desired color.

NOTE. The Miniature Flower-boxes as shown on the table in the Dining-room Interior are made with the legs projecting ⅝ of an inch above the top of the box as well as 1¼ inches below.

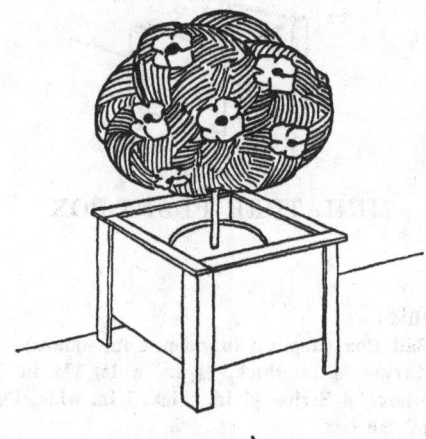

JARDINIÈRE

Illustration 8 *Figures 1 and 2*

Requirements:

Body. 1 Butter Box (about 10¼ in. deep, 13¾ in. wide, 14¼ in. long).

Legs. 4 Strips ½ in. thick, 1½ in. wide, 4 in. longer than depth of the box. 4 Strips ½ in. thick, 2 in. wide, 4 in. longer than depth of the box.

Facing Strips. 2 Strips ½ in. thick, 2 in. wide, 1½ in. longer than outside width of the box. 2 Strips ½ in. thick, 2 in. wide, 1½ in. longer than outside length of the box.

Construction:

Make the legs 4 inches longer than the depth of the box with the cover removed.

Remove the cover of the box and nail the legs to each corner, keeping the tops of the legs even with the top of the sides of the box. Cut the ends of the facing strips perfectly square and nail them in place, as shown in illustration, allowing their inside edges to project ¼ of an inch over the inside face of the sides of the box.

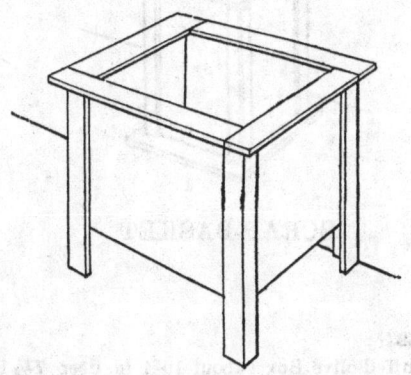

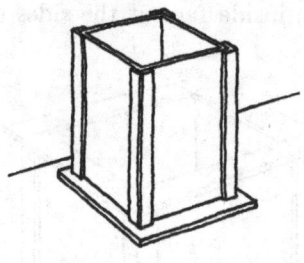

SCRAP-BASKET

Illustration 9   *Figure 1*

Requirements:

Body. 1 Stuffed-olive Box (about 10¾ in. deep, 7½ in. square).

Corner Trim. 4 Strips ¼ in. thick, 1 in. wide, and length equal to height of the box. 4 Strips ¼ in. thick, 1¼ in. wide, and length equal to height of the box.

False Bottom. 1 Piece ½ in. thick, 4 in. greater square than the box.

Construction:

Remove the cover or top end from box. Make the length of corner trim equal to height of the box. Turn the box bottom up and place the false bottom or base upon it, allowing the bottom to project 2 inches all around; and secure it by nailing through it and into the edges of the four sides. If the sides are too thin to receive the nails, nail through the real bottom and clinch the nails on the inside. Set the heads of the nails well in, so they will be at least even with the bottom of the face. Invert the box, placing it upon its new base. Measure and cut each corner trim the exact height of each corner. Nail a corner trim to each corner and clinch the nails on the inside if they project. Sandpaper and fill imperfections with putty, and stain if desired.

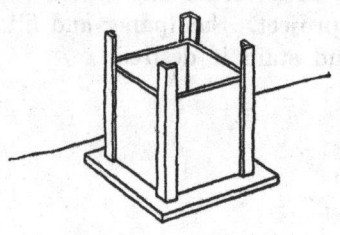

SCRAP-BOX

Illustration 10   *Figure 1*

Requirements:

Body. 1 Stuffed-olive Box (about 10¾ in. deep, 7½ in. square).

Corner Trim. 4 Strips ⅜ in. thick, 1 in. wide, 2½ in. longer than height of the box. 4 Strips ⅜ in. thick, 1⅜ in. wide, 2½ in. longer than height of the box.

False Bottom. 1 Piece ½ in. thick, 4 in. larger than the box each way.

Construction:

Remove the cover from the box. Make the corner trim 2½ inches longer than the height of the box. Proceed as in Illustration No. 9 until ready to put the corner trim in place. Each corner trim should project 2½ inches above the top of the box.

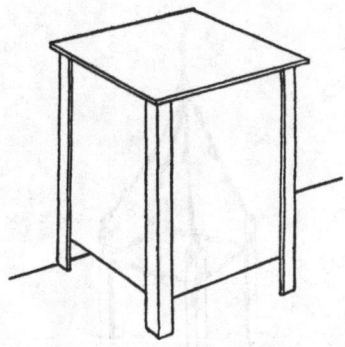

KITCHEN STOOL

Illustration 11   *Figure 1*

Requirements:

Body. 1 Olive-oil Box (about 14 in. deep and 9¾ in. square).

Top. 1 Piece ¾ in. thick, 3 in. wider than the outside of the square end.

Legs. 4 Strips ⅜ in. thick, 1⅝ in. wide, 16 in. long. 4 Strips ⅜ in. thick, 1¾ in. wide, 16 in. long.

Construction:

Make the legs 16 inches long. Remove the cover from the box. Turn the box bottom up and nail the top on, allowing it to project 1½ inches all around. Use 1½ inch brads and set their heads in slightly below the top face. Invert the box and nail a leg on each corner, setting the upper ends of the legs against the under side of the top.

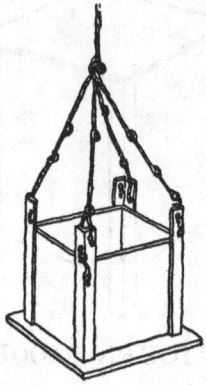

HANGING FLOWER-BOX

Illustration 12   *Figures 1 and 2*

Requirements:

Same as for Scrap-box, Illustration No. 10, with the addition of 30 feet of ordinary clothes-line.

Construction:

Proceed the same as described for the construction of the scrap-box. Bore three ½ inch holes in that part of the leg projecting above the top of the box, one hole in one face and two holes in the other face of each leg, all located at different levels as shown by knots in the illustration. The rope is knotted on each side of the holes to hide them. Make a variety of knots, using two in some and three in others, thus giving the desired artistic effect, as the charm of hanging boxes depends largely upon that novel and simple method of hanging. Knot the ropes at uneven intervals as you will, without regard to any rule, so long as you obtain the desired effect.

NOTE. The Hanging Flower-boxes shown in the Living-room Interior are two of these boxes, each hung from an end of a rope, which is suspended, and slides over two hooks, and as one plant is drawn down to be watered, the other plant rises.

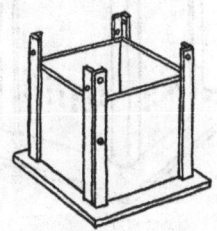

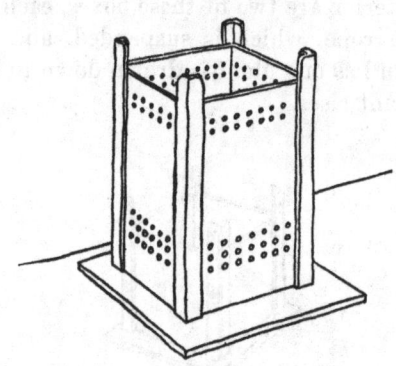

PERFORATED SCRAP-BOX

Illustration 13 *Figure 1*

Requirements:
Same as for the Scrap-box, Illustration No. 10.

Construction:
Same as described for the scrap-box, after which perforate as follows: Bore two rows of holes ½ inch in diameter through each side near the top, and three rows of holes near the bottom, spaced apart equally, about 1 inch from center to center.

BOX FURNITURE 37

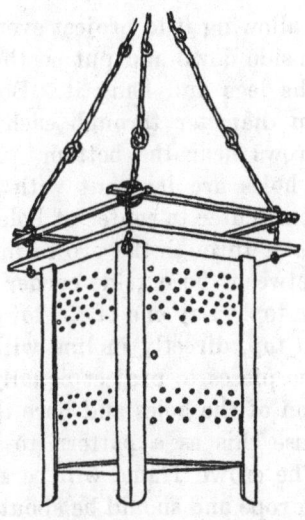

HANGING LANTERN
Illustration 14 *Figure 1*

Requirements:
Body. 1 Olive-oil Box (about 14¼ in. deep, 9¾ in. square).

Legs. 4 Strips ⅜ in. thick, 1⅛ in. wide, 4 in. longer than height of the box. 4 Strips ⅜ in. thick, 1½ in. wide, 4 in. longer than height of the box.

Top. 1 Piece ½ in. thick, 2 in. larger each way than the end of the box.

Crown Frame. 4 Pieces ½ in. thick, 2 in. wide, 8 in. longer than the outside width of the box.

26 ft. of ordinary clothes-line.

Construction:
Make the corner trim 4 inches longer than the length of the box. Remove one side. Place the box on end and

nail the top on, allowing it to project evenly on all sides. Turn the box upside down and put on the legs. Fit the door between the legs and hang it. Bore six rows of holes ½ inch in diameter through each side, near the top, and four rows near the bottom. Care should be taken that the holes are laid out with equal spaces— about 1 inch from center to center of holes. Bore a hole ½ inch in diameter through the projecting corner of the top, half-way between the outside corner of the leg and the corner of the top. Lay one of the lower pieces of the corner frame on top, directly in line with the holes, allowing the frame pieces to project equally over the top. Mark the position of the holes and bore them ½ inch in diameter, and use this as a pattern to bore the other three pieces. The crown frame will be suspended by a knot tied in each rope and should be about 3 inches above the top of the lantern. The same artistic features of hanging should be observed as are described for the Hanging Flower-box, Illustration No. 12.

CHAPTER III

THE SAME PRINCIPLES AS CHAPTER II WITH THE ADDITION OF CIRCULAR CUTS

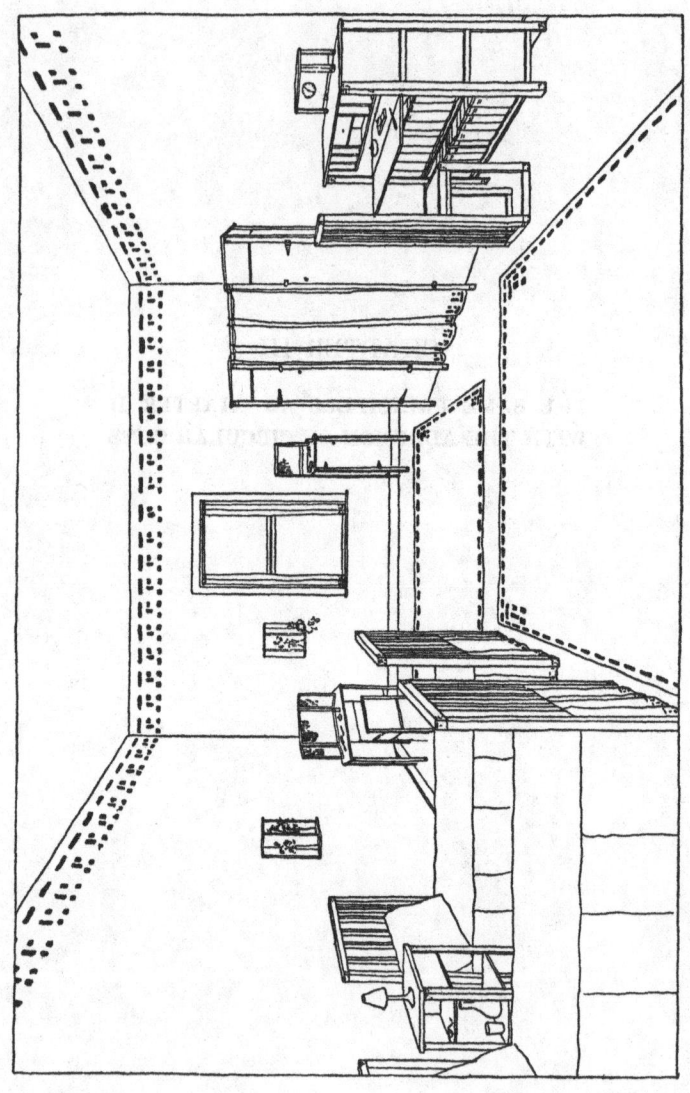

Twin-Bed Room

TWIN-BED TABLE   VASE WALL BRACKETS
TRIPLE-MIRROR DRESSING-TABLE AND CHAIR
"SHAVINGETTE"
COMBINATION WASHSTAND AND WARDROBE
BOOKCASE DESK   OBLONG CLOCK

The desk chair is not made from boxes.

Color Scheme:
    Gray (dark and light).
    White.

Woodwork:
    Neutral gray (paint).

Furniture:
    Neutral gray, with motif stenciled in white.

Walls:
    Neutral gray, with motif stenciled in white and old rose, or white and lavender.

Ceiling:
    White.

Hangings and Bed Coverings:
    French gray colored linen, with motif appliquéd or embroidered same color as stencil on wall.

Curtains:
    White muslin.

Floor:
    Painted gray; rugs light and dark gray, with shade of old rose or lavender in the border.

Plants:
    Cut flowers or growing plants with either old rose, lavender, or white blossoms.

CHAPTER III

Illustration 15

FOOTSTOOL

Box turned upside down; cover removed, otherwise left intact. Legs and false top added.

Illustration 16

COAL- OR PAPER-BOX

Box placed top side up; cover removed, otherwise left intact. Legs and false top added.

Illustration 17

BLACKING-BOX

Box placed top side up; cover removed, otherwise left intact. Legs and folding false top with sole block added.

Illustration 18

OBLONG CLOCK CASE

Box placed on side; cover removed and hinged as a door, oval sawed from the bottom. Legs and false top added.

Illustration 19

UPRIGHT CLOCK CASE

Box placed on end; cover removed and hinged as a door, oval sawed from the bottom. Legs and false top added.

Illustration 20

NURSERY CLOCK CASE

Box placed on end; cover and one end removed. New cover added.

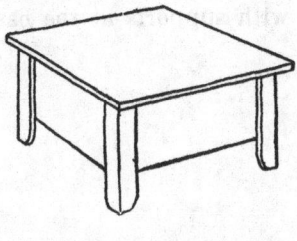

FOOTSTOOL

Illustration 15 *Figure 1*

Requirements:
Body. 1 Roach-food Box (about 5 in. deep, 10 in. square).

Top. 1 Piece ¾ in. thick, square 2 in. greater than the box.

Legs. 4 Pieces ⅜ in. thick, 1⅜ in. wide, 6½ in. long. 4 Pieces ⅜ in. thick, 1¾ in. wide, 6½ in. long.

Construction:
Make the legs 6½ inches long and round off the corners of one end of each leg, otherwise the constant moving about of the stool will have a tendency to split off the sharp corners.

Remove the cover. Turn the box upside down and nail a leg on each corner and clinch the nails on the inside.

Invert the box, set it upon the legs, and place the false top on it, allowing an even projection on each side, and nail it securely near the edges.

NOTE 1. The stool by the bedside in the Nursery Interior is an inverted box on legs similar to the footstool, the legs being longer and the box of less depth than the footstool.

NOTE 2. The stools in the Club-room Interior are made the same, with supports at the base.

BOX FURNITURE   45

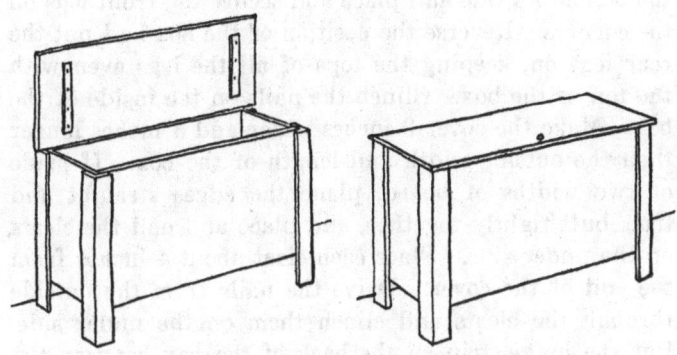

COAL- OR PAPER-BOX

Illustration 16 *Figures 1 and 2*

Requirements:

Body. 1 Small Packing Box (about 14 in. deep, 16 in. wide, 27 in. long).

Cover. 1 Piece ½ in. thick, 3 in. wider than the width of the box, 3 in. longer than the length of the box (outside measurements).

Cleats. 2 Strips ½ in. thick, 2 in. wide, and the length 2 in. shorter than the inside width of the box.

Hardware. 1 Pair of 2 in. iron hinges (butts) with screws ⅝ in. long.

Legs. 4 Strips ½ in. thick, 1½ in. wide, 4 in. longer than the depth of the box. 4 Strips ½ in. thick, 2 in. wide, 4 in. longer than the depth of the box.

Hinge-strip. 1 Strip ½ in. thick, 2 in. wide, 3 in. shorter than the outside length of the box.

Construction:

Make the legs 4 inches longer than the depth of the box with the cover removed. Remove the cover. Turn the box on its side and place and secure the front legs on the corners. Reverse the position of the box and put the rear legs on, keeping the tops of all the legs even with the top of the box. Clinch the nails on the inside of the box. Make the cover 3 inches wider and 3 inches longer than the outside width and length of the box. If made of two widths of board, plane the edges straight and true, butt tightly together, and place and nail the cleats on the under side. Place each cleat about 4 inches from the end of the cover. Drive the nails from the outside through the cleats and clinch them on the under side. Put the hinge-strip on the back of the box between the legs, keeping its top edge even with the top edge of the back of the box. Set the cover in place, with an even projection all around. Place the hinges so one half can be screwed to the under side of the projecting back edge of the cover, and the other half to the hinge-strip on the back of the box, thus:

The hinges may be set about 6 inches from each end of the box. Sandpaper and fill imperfections, and color as desired.

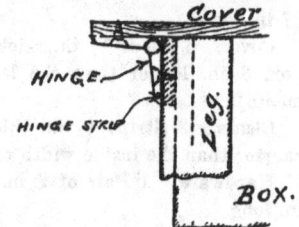

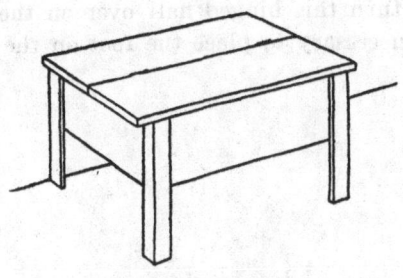

BLACKING-BOX

Illustration 17   *Figure 1*

Requirements:

Body. 1 Butter Box (about 5¾ in. deep, 13¾ in. wide, 14¼ in. long).

Top. Two Pieces ½ in. thick, 1½ in. wider than one half the outside width of the box, by 3 in. longer than the outside length of the box.

Legs. 4 Strips ⅜ in. thick, 1⅜ in. wide, by 7 in. longer than the outside depth of the box. 4 Strips ⅜ in. thick, 1¾ in. wide, by 7 in. longer than the outside depth of the box.

Sole Block. 1 Block 2 in. thick, shaped like the sole of a shoe.

Hardware. 2 1½ in. hinges (butts) and screws.

Construction:

Make the legs 7 inches longer than the outside depth of the box. Remove the cover. Turn the box on end and nail on the legs. Stand it right side up on the legs; nail on one half the cover, allowing it to project evenly on the side and ends. Hang the other half of cover, placing the hinges in the joint between each half cover. Cut the edges of each half cover to let the hinges in even. Nail the sole block on the under side of the hinged half of the cover, and turn this hinged half over on the fixed half when it is necessary to place the foot on the sole block.

OBLONG CLOCK CASE

Illustration 18   *Figure 1*

Requirements:

Body. 1 Gelatin Box (about 4 in. deep, 8 in. wide, 10 in. long).

Top. 1 Piece ½ in. thick, 2 in. wider than the outside depth of the box, 2 in. longer than the length of the box outside.

Legs. 4 Strips ¼ in. thick, 1 in. wide, 1½ in. longer than the width of the box outside. 4 Strips ¼ in. thick, 1¼ in. wide, 1½ in. longer than the width of the box outside.

Hardware. 2 ⅞ in. brass hinges (butts) and screws. 1 brass hook, screw-eye, and screw.

Construction:

Make the legs 1½ inches longer than the width of the box. Remove the cover. Place the box on its side and nail the top in place, allowing it to project 1 inch all around. Secure the legs on each corner. With the keyhole-saw cut a circular opening in the center of the bottom of the box, which is now to become the face of the Clock Case. This opening is to be made of a diameter to fit the face of the clock. Measure the clock face and with a pair of dividers inscribe a circle as a guide. Cut the opening a little smaller than desired. Sandpaper smooth the edges of the hole to the correct size. From the cover removed, make a door to fit the space between the legs and lower edge of the case to the under side of the top. Hang it on the hinges and use hook and screw-eye to fasten it. Set the clock in place and, if necessary, place a small block on the bottom inside for supporting at the right level.

This is especially adapted for the ordinary American alarm-clock, which is sold at a very low price.

UPRIGHT CLOCK CASE

Illustration 19 *Figure 1*

Requirements:

Body. 1 Gelatin Box (about 4 in. deep, 8 in. wide, 10 in. long).

Top. 1 Piece ½ in. thick, 2 in. wider than the outside depth of the box, 2 in. longer than the outside width of the box.

Legs. 4 Strips ¼ in. thick, 1 in. wide, 2 in. longer than the outside length of the box. 4 Strips ¼ in. thick, 1¼ in. wide, 2 in. longer than the outside length of the box.

Hardware. 2 ⅞ in. brass hinges (butts) and screws. 1 brass hook, screw-eye, and screw.

Construction:

Make the legs 2 inches longer than the outside length of the box. Remove the cover. Place the box on its end and nail the top in place, allowing its edges to project evenly about 1 inch all around. Invert the box, turning the other end up, and nail on the legs. Measure the diameter of the face of the clock to be used, and, with the dividers, inscribe a circle ¼ inch smaller in diameter on the original bottom of the box, which is now to be the face of the clock case, placing the center of the circle 6 inches from the lower end of the case. With a keyhole-saw cut around on the circle. Sandpaper smooth the edges of the hole to the correct size. From the cover removed, make a door to fit the case between the legs on the back, keeping the outer face of the door and the outer face of the legs even. Hang the door upon the hinges and screw on the hook and eye to fasten it. Set the clock in place and put a small shelf or block under it to support it at the right level.

BOX FURNITURE 53

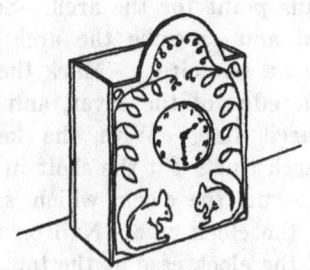

NURSERY CLOCK CASE
Illustration 20   *Figure 1*

Requirements:
Body. 1 Extract of Beef Box (about 3½ in. deep, 7¼ in. wide, 9 in. long).

One Shelf. 1 Piece ⅜ in. thick, width and length to fit inside the box.

Construction:
Remove the cover and one end. Make a cover 11 inches long from a portion of another box. Five and three quarter inches from one end on the center line of the cover will be the center for the hole which is to be cut that the clock dial may be seen. With a pair of dividers inscribe a circle to suit the size of the face of the clock and bore a hole, about ½ inch in diameter, inside the circle. The outer edge of the hole should be on the circle line. Insert the keyhole-saw in the small opening and cut on the line of the circle completely around, and sandpaper true and smooth the edges after

the circular piece is removed. Eight and a half inches from the same end and on the center line of the cover will be the radius point for the arch. Set the dividers 2½ inches open and describe the arch line, which is slightly less than a semicircle. Mark the length of the box on each side edge of the cover, and cut from that point to the arch line. With the keyhole-saw cut around on the arch line. Fit the shelf in the box at the proper height to suit the clock, which will stand upon the shelf inside the clock case. Nail on the cover with the open end of the clock case at the top. Set the clock upon the shelf through the open top end of the case. The face of the clock case can be made quite a pleasing feature by the use of an appropriate design.

CHAPTER IV

THE BOX TAKEN PARTIALLY APART SO THAT IT LOSES ITS ORIGINAL SHAPE

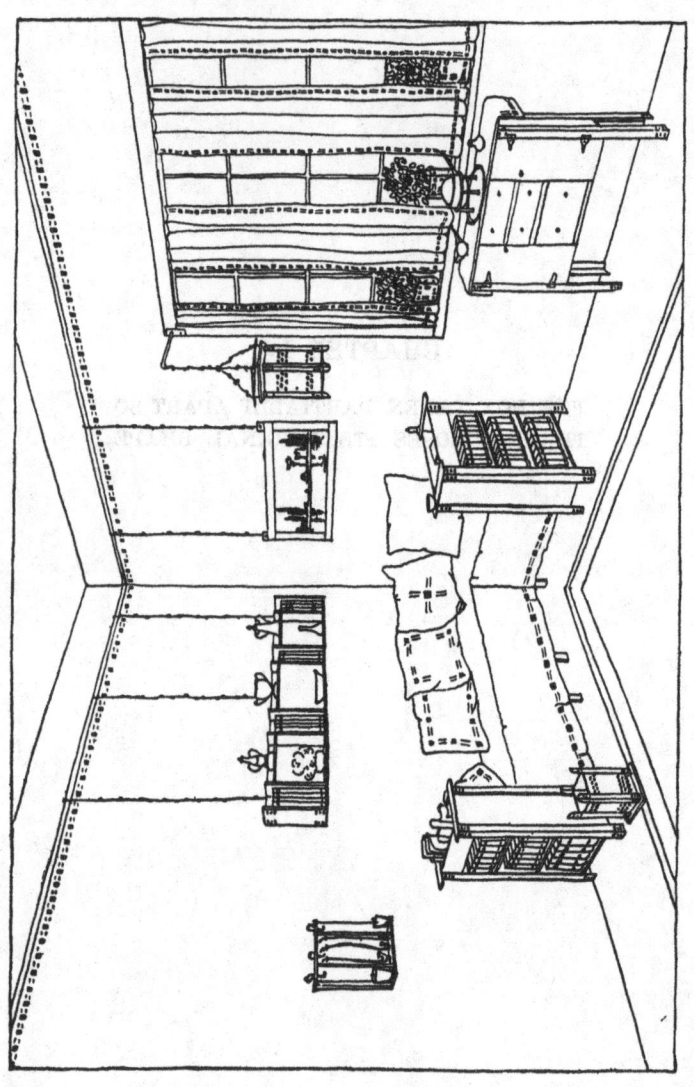

The College Boy's Corner

PIPE RACK   PERFORATED SCRAP-BOX   FLAG WALL RACK
COLLEGE CORNER SEAT   PICTURE FRAME NO. 1
HANGING LANTERN
CHAFING-DISH STAND   PLANT-BOX

Color Scheme:
   Mission oak (dark tan).
   Olive green.

Woodwork:
   Mission oak.

Furniture:
   Mission oak.

Walls:
   Olive green, with motif stenciled in same color as furniture.

Ceiling:
   Deep cream.

Hangings and Corner-Seat Covering:
   Burlap the same color as walls, with motif stenciled in same color as furniture.

Pillows:
   Burlap in olive green, old gold, old blues and tans, with motif stenciled in same color as furniture.

Curtains:
   Net of deep cream color, with motif stenciled or embroidered in same color as furniture.

Floor:
   Painted or stained same color as furniture.

Plants:
   Growing ivy, or plants with either crimson, bachelor's button, yellow, or cream-white blossoms.

CHAPTER IV

Illustration 21
SMALL WALL RACK
Box placed on side, cover removed. Sides set in.

Illustration 22
WALL BRACKET
Box placed on side, cover removed. Ends set in.

Illustration 23
VASE WALL BRACKET
Box placed on end, cover removed. Sides set in.

Illustration 24
KITCHEN SPICE-BOX
Box placed on end, cover removed and used for shelves. Sides set in.

Illustration 25
PIPE RACK
The Vase Wall Bracket, with the top perforated.

Illustration 26
HOUSEWIFE'S HANDY RACK NO. 1
The Small Wall Rack, with the upper shelf perforated.

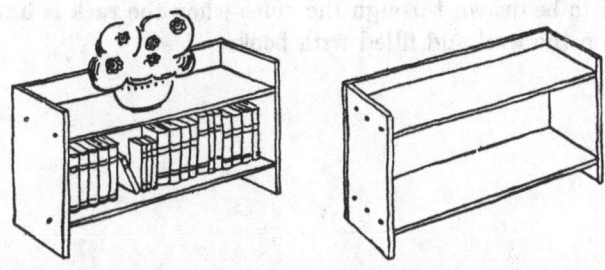

SMALL WALL RACK

Illustration 21 *Figures 1 and 2*

Requirements:

Body. 1 Condensed-milk Box (about 7¼ in. deep, 13 in. wide, 19¾ in. long).

Hardware. 2 picture hooks and picture wire.

Construction:

Remove the cover carefully and put it aside for future use. Take off both sides by withdrawing the nails, and cut off each end of the sides, making them the exact length of the box inside. Draw a pencil line across the bottom and up each end, 2½ inches from the side edges. Set the sides in, keeping their outside faces on the pencil line, and secure them by nails driven through each end and through the bottom. Plane off all the edges necessary to make them even with each other, using sandpaper afterward to remove any objectionable blemishes or inequalities. Bore a hole ⅛ inch in diameter in the center of each end, 4 inches down from the top edge of the rack. Insert the hanging wires through the holes from the outside, and knot their ends tightly and sufficiently large not to be drawn through the holes when the rack is hung upon the wall and filled with books.

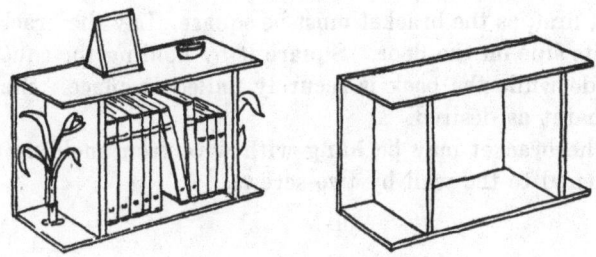

WALL BRACKET

Illustration 22 *Figures 1 and 2*

Requirements:

Body. 1 Condensed-milk Box (about 7¼ in. deep, 13 in. wide, 19¾ in. long).

Hardware. 2 picture hooks and picture wire.

Construction:

Remove the cover carefully and put aside for future use.

If possible, withdraw all the nails from the ends of the box without marring the sides. Otherwise, take the box apart by first removing the bottom, then the sides.

If any portions are rough or bear objectionable brands or blemishes, either plane or sandpaper them smooth while the parts are separated and the nails removed.

Draw a pencil line across the best face of each of the sides 4 inches from each end. Set the ends in, keeping the outside face of the ends exactly to the line, and nail each side to the ends, using care to keep all the edges even with each other. Draw a line across the best face of the bottom 4 inches from each end, and then put the bottom on, driving the nails in just far enough to tack it at first, as the bracket must be square. Lay the bracket on its side on the floor. Square it by holding the square inside while the back is securely nailed in place. Stain or paint as desired.

The bracket may be hung with wire from molding or fastened to the wall by two screws.

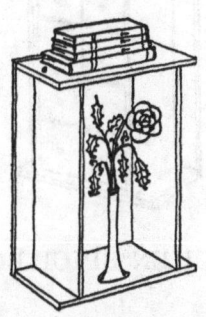

VASE WALL BRACKET

Illustration 23 *Figure 1*

Requirements:

The same as for the Small Wall Rack, shown in Illustration No. 21.

Construction:

The same as described for the Small Wall Rack, Illustration No. 21, with the single exception that the bracket is hung from one end only, the holes being bored 4 inches from the back and 2 inches from the side edge. The wire knots are on the under side of the top of the bracket.

KITCHEN SPICE-BOX

Illustration 24 *Figure 1*

Requirements:

Body. 1 Peanut-butter Box (about 4¾ in. deep, 12½ in. wide, 18¼ in. long). 8 Salt Boxes (about 4 in. deep, 4 in. wide, 4 in. long).

Shelves. 3 Pieces ⅜ in. thick, as wide as the inside depth of the large box, and 8¼ in. long.

Construction:

Make the rack the same as described for the Small Wall Rack, Illustration No. 21.

Fit and nail the shelves in place, spacing them equal distances apart, thus making four compartments of equal size. Place the rack on end and hang it in that position on the wall.

Place two of the small boxes in each compartment and put the spices in them.

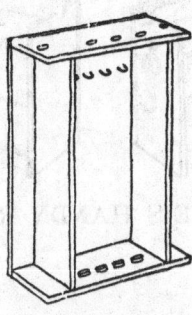

PIPE RACK

Illustration 25   *Figure 1*

Requirements:

The same as for the Small Wall Rack, Illustration No. 21.

Construction:

Make the same as the Small Wall Rack, Illustration No. 21, and turn the rack on end.

Bore the five holes in the top end ½ inch in diameter for receiving the stems of short pipes. Gouge depressions ½ inch deep on the inside face of the bottom end to receive the bowls of the long pipes. Drive staples into the inside face of the back at such heights as are best adapted to the various long pipes.

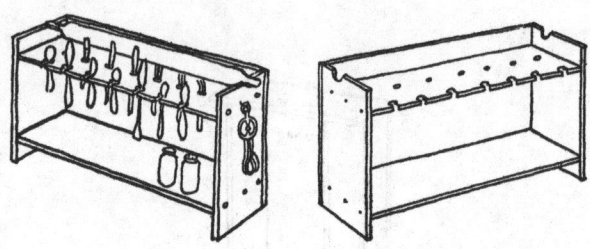

HOUSEWIFE'S HANDY RACK No. 1

Illustration 26   *Figures 1 and 2*

Requirements:

Body. 1 Condensed-milk Box (about 7¼ in. deep, 13 in. wide, 19¾ in. long).

Hardware. Picture wire and hooks.

Construction:

Make body of the rack the same as described for the Small Wall Rack, Illustration No. 21.

Bore two rows of holes ¾ inch in diameter, spaced about 2 inches from center to center. The center of the front row of holes is ¾ inch and the center of the second row 2½ inches back from the front edge of the rack. Cut slots ¼ inch wide from the front edge to the front row of holes.

About half-way between the rear row of holes and the back of the rack, gouge out the top of each end of the rack to fit the handle of the rolling-pin. Hang with picture hooks and wire, or nail to the wall, as desired.

CHAPTER V

COMBINATIONS OF CHAPTER IV

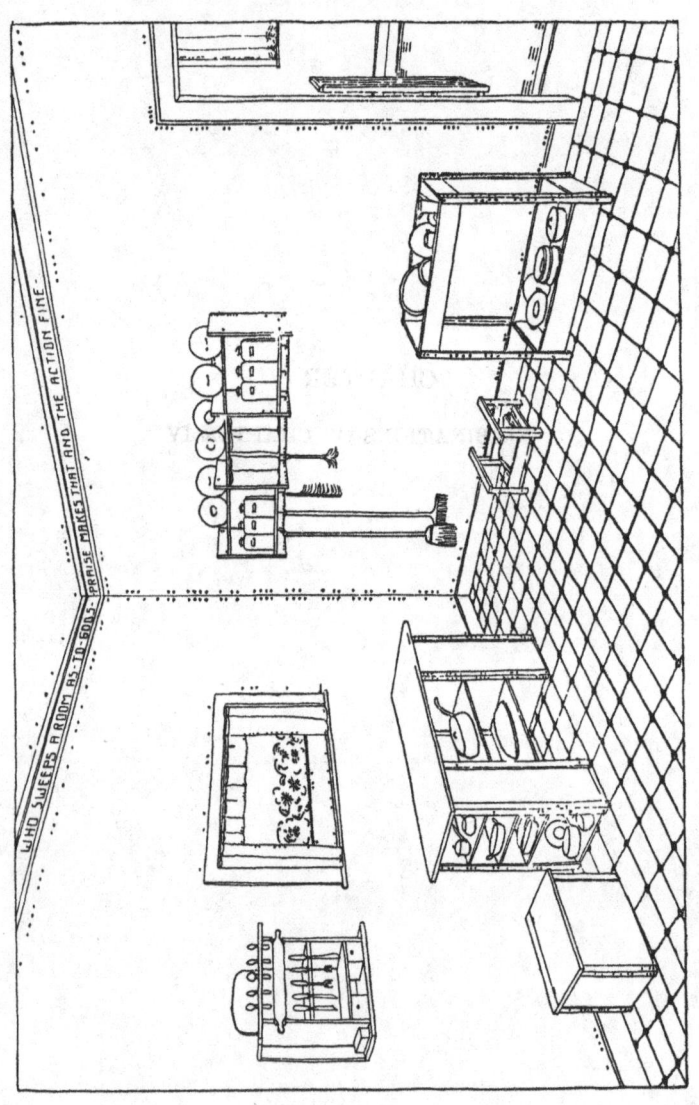

The Kitchen

HOUSEWIFE'S HANDY RACK NO. 3
ROLLING SOILED-DISH TABLE   PAPER-BOX
BROOM SHELF
KITCHEN TABLE   NEWSPAPER RACK

Color Scheme:
    White.
    Blue (the color of your agate ware).

Woodwork:
    White paint.

Furniture:
    White paint, with motif stenciled in blue.

Walls:
    White, with motif and motto stenciled in blue.

Ceiling:
    White.

Curtains:
    White cotton, with motif appliquéd in blue.

Aprons and Kitchen Dresses:
    Same shade of blue, or white.

Floor:
    Blue and white oilcloth or linoleum.

Plants:
    Growing parsley and plants with white blossoms.

CHAPTER V

Illustration 27

KITCHEN COMFORT

Two boxes placed upon sides, one upon the other; covers removed (one used as shelf), otherwise left intact.

Illustration 28

DOUBLE WALL RACK

Two Small Wall Racks in combination. Facing strips added.

Illustration 29

LARGE WALL BOOK RACK

Three Small Wall Racks in combination. Facing strips added.

Illustration 30

WALL BOOK AND KNICKKNACK BRACKET

One Small Wall Rack and two Wall Brackets in combination. Facing strips and false top added.

Illustration 31

HOUSEWIFE'S HANDY RACK NO. 2

Two Wall Brackets in combination. The two upper shelves perforated.

Illustration 32

MAGAZINE RACK

Three boxes turned on end; covers removed and used as shelves. Legs and false top added.

Illustration 33

SHOE CUPBOARD

The Magazine Rack with doors added.

Illustration 34

HOUSEWIFE'S HANDY RACK NO. 3

Box placed on end; cover removed and used as shelves. Two upper shelves perforated. Drawers added.

BOX FURNITURE 71

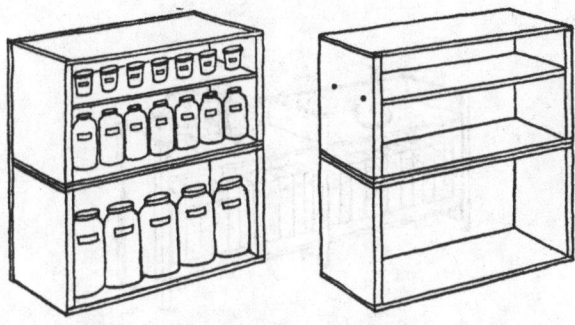

KITCHEN COMFORT

Illustration 27 *Figures 1 and 2*

Requirements:

Body. 2 Condensed-milk Boxes (about 7¼ in. deep, 13 in. wide, 19¾ in. long).

Shelf. 1 Piece ½ in. thick, width equal to the inside depth of the box, and length equal to the inside length of the box.

Construction:

Remove the covers of both boxes, reserving one cover from which to cut the shelf.

Place one box upon the other, as shown in the illustration. Secure them together by nailing through the lower side of the upper box and the upper side of the lower box, and clinch the nails underneath. In doing so, drive the nails near the edges, to insure solidity. Keep the boxes perfectly matched while nailing. Cut the shelf to the neat inside length and nail it in, keeping its under side 1 inch higher than the top of the pint jars. Secure it by driving nails through each end of the box into the ends of the shelf.

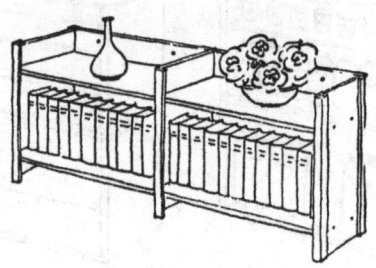

DOUBLE WALL RACK

Illustration 28   *Figure 1*

Requirements:

Body. 2 Condensed-milk Boxes (about 7¼ in. deep, 13 in. wide, 19¾ in. long).

Facing Strips. 3 Strips ⅜ in. thick, 1½ in. wide, and length equal to the inside width of the box.

Construction:

Make two Small Wall Racks as described for Illustration No. 21. Stand one rack on its end and place the other rack upon it endwise, with both compartments facing the same way. Match their edges and nail them together.

Nail the facing strips on the vertical edge faces, allowing the middle one to project evenly on each side, and having the outside edge of the end ones even with the end of the rack.

LARGE WALL BOOK RACK

Illustration 29 *Figure 1*

Requirements:

Body. 3 Condensed-milk Boxes (about 7¼ in. deep, 13 in. wide, 19¾ in. long).

Facing Strips. 4 Strips ⅜ in. thick, 1¾ in. wide, as long as the inside width of the box.

Construction:

This rack is a combination of three small racks as shown for Small Wall Rack, Illustration No. 21.

Make three small racks as described therein, all of equal size.

Place one rack on end upon the floor, then place the second one on this, also endwise. Secure the ends together by driving the nails from the inside of the top bracket and clinch them on the under side. Place the third rack on the second and secure it in the same manner. Care must be exercised to keep the edges even with each other and have all three brackets, when joined, form a straight line.

Place the facing strips on the front face of the ends to cover joints as shown, the outer edge of end strip to be even with the outside face of the rack; ⅛ inch holes may be bored through the back face, as shown in the illustration. The rack may be hung with wire from a molding.

NOTE. The Broom Shelf shown in the Kitchen Interior is the Large Wall Rack with a curtain, and hooks added underneath on which to hang the brooms and aprons.

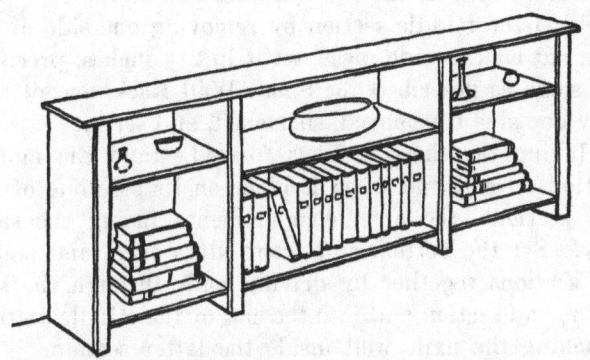

WALL BOOK AND KNICKKNACK BRACKET

Illustration 30 *Figures 1 and 2*

Requirements:

Body. 3 Condensed-milk Boxes (about 7¼ in. deep, 13 in. wide, 19¾ in. long).

Top. 1 Board ⅝ in. thick, 49 in. long.

Facing Strips. 4 Strips ⅜ in. thick, 1½ in. wide.

Construction:

This construction combines principles in Small Wall Rack, Illustration No. 21, and Wall Bracket, Illustration No. 22. The two end compartments are formed of boxes with their ends set in, similar to those in the Wall Bracket, while the middle section is a partial adaptation of that shown for Small Wall Rack.

To form the end sections, proceed as described for the Wall Bracket, except in this case draw the lines so that one end of each box will set in 2½ inches, while the other end will set in 8 inches. The latter in the completed rack forms the shelf in each end section.

Form the middle section by removing one side of the box, cut off this side piece, set it in 2½ inches, precisely the same as described for Small Wall Rack, except that only one side is removed, shortened, and set in.

Having the three sections formed, stand the middle section on end and upon it place on its side one of the end sections, the open compartments facing the same way. Set the bottom and front edges even, and secure the sections together by driving nails through the side of the end section and into the end of the middle section, clinching the nails well inside the latter section.

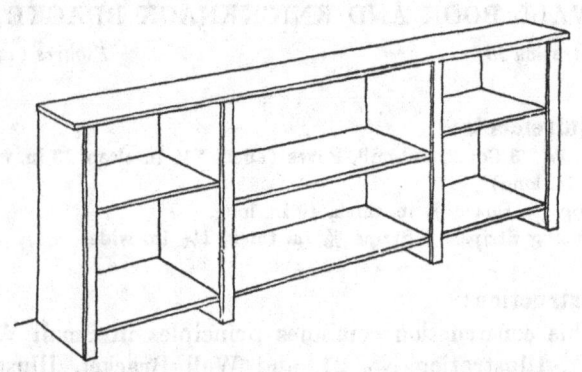

Reverse them, placing the side of the end section upon the floor, with the blank end of the middle section up. Set the other end section upon this and secure them in the same manner. Set the bracket upon the floor, right side up, just as it would hang on the wall. Place the top on with rear edge even with the back of the bracket, and mark and cut it so that it will project 1½ inches over each end and front edge of bracket, and nail it in position securely. Measure and cut the facing strips and nail them in place, keeping the outside edge of the end ones even with the end of the bracket.

The bracket may be hung upon four picture cords suspended from hooks on the molding, or in any way best adapted to the surroundings.

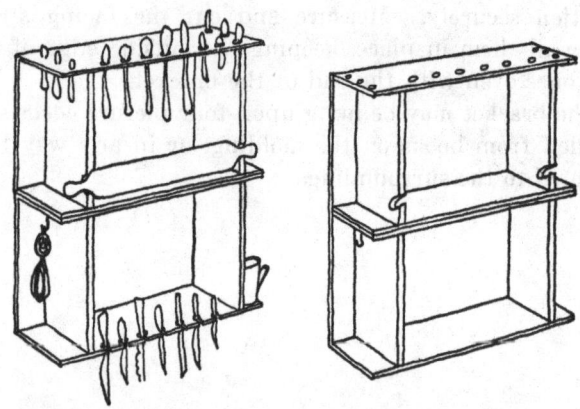

HOUSEWIFE'S HANDY RACK No. 2

Illustration 31   *Figures 1 and 2*

Requirements:

Body. 2 Condensed-milk Boxes (about 7¼ in. deep, 13 in. wide, 19¾ in. long).

Hardware. 2 picture hooks and picture wire.

Construction:

Remove the covers carefully for future use. Withdraw all the nails from the end of one box without marring the sides or bottom any more than is necessary. Move the end in so that the sides and bottom will project 4 inches beyond the outside face of the end. Nail the sides and bottom to the end. Do the same with the other end of the same box, and it will then look like the lower half of the illustration. Do the same thing with the other box, and they will be ready to join together.

Turn one box on its side and place the other box on its side upon the first, the open sides facing in the same direction. Match their edges and nail them together, driving the nails from the inside of the upper compartment, through both thicknesses, into the lower compartment and clinch them.

In each end, 1 inch from the front edge and 2 inches from the bottom of compartment, bore a hole large enough to receive the handle of the rolling-pin. Saw a slightly slanting slot of the same width as the diameter of the hole from the front edge of the end to the outer edge of the hole, and trim off slightly the sharp edges and sandpaper smooth. Do the same in the other end and fit the rolling-pin in.

Bore suitable holes for receiving the handles of the spoons through the top of the rack, say about 1 inch from edge to center of the holes, and fit the spoons in them. Bore holes in the bottom of the rack to suit the smallest part of the knife handles, the same distance from the edge. Saw slots $\frac{1}{4}$ inch wide from edge to the hole to pass the knife blades, and fit the knives in. Small brass hooks may be put in convenient places for various articles.

The rack may be hung from the molding with picture hooks and wire, or, if more convenient, fastened through the back to the wall with screws.

BOX FURNITURE

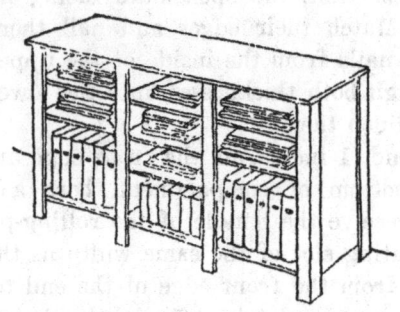

MAGAZINE RACK

Illustration 32 *Figure 1*

Requirements:

Body. 3 Washing-soap Boxes (about 11¾ in. deep, 14¼ in. wide, 20 in. long).

Top. 1 Piece ½ in. thick, 1¾ in. wider than the depth of the box with the cover removed, and 2¾ in. longer than three times the outside width of the box.

Legs. 4 Strips ⅜ in. thick, 1½ in. wide, and 4 in. longer than the outside length of the box. 4 Strips ⅜ in. thick, 2 in. wide, and 4 in. longer than the outside length of the box.

Facing Strips. 4 Strips ⅜ in. thick, 2 in. wide, and 4 in. longer than the outside length of the box.

Shelves. 7 Pieces ½ in. thick, width equal to the inside depth of the box, and length equal to the inside width of the box. A portion can be made from the covers removed.

Cleats. 14 Strips ½ in. thick, 1½ in. wide, and length equal to the inside depth of the box. 6 Strips ½ in. thick, 1½ in. wide 4 in. shorter than the inside width of the box.

Construction:

Make the legs 4 inches longer than the outside length of the box. Remove the covers. Lay one box on its side and another on its side on top of the first box. Secure them together by nailing through the abutting sides. On top of the second box place the third and secure it in the same manner. Clinch the nails on the inside, having the open compartments all face the same way. Space the shelves to suit height of the books. The under side of the shelf will be the top line of the cleat. Mark on each side of each compartment these top lines and nail the cleats in place. Place and secure the false top, keeping its rear edge even with the rear outside face of the back legs, allowing it to project at the ends and in front 1 inch over the outside face of the legs. Nail it securely near the outer edges. Nail the corner legs and the rear facing strips in place, and then fit the shelves and put in place upon the cleats. The shelves need not be secured at all, and can be readily emptied, removed, and cleaned when necessary.

SHOE CUPBOARD

Illustration 33 *Figures 1 and 2*

Requirements:

Same as for Magazine Rack, Illustration No. 32, with the addition of doors, etc., also as follows:

Doors. 3 Pieces ½ in. thick, the width 2 in. less than the outside width of the box, and length equal to the outside length of the box.

Cleats. 6 Strips ½ in. thick, 2 in. wide, about 1 ft. long to cut for door cleats.

Hardware. 6 1½ in. iron hinges (butts) with screws which come with them. 3 small door pull-knobs. 3 brass buttons and screws.

Construction:

Proceed the same as for Magazine Rack. Fit the doors and put the cleats on about 3 inches from each end. They must be so placed as to clear the shelves when door is closed. Mark on the doors the position of the hinges, say about 4 inches from both top and bottom; cut out the edge of the door enough to let one side of the hinges in even. Set the door in place and mark the leg and cut that in a similar way. Screw the hinges to the door, then set the door up and screw to the leg. The outside face of the doors will be even with the face of the legs. Place the pull-knobs about one third the distance down from the top of the door and 2 inches from the edge. Screw the buttons on the facing strips at the same height as the pull-knobs.

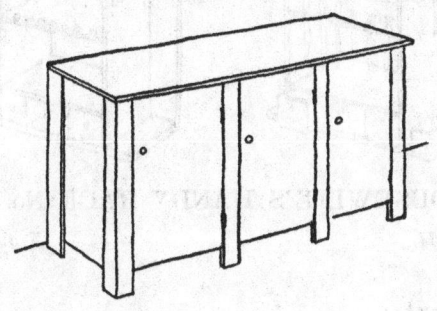

BOX FURNITURE

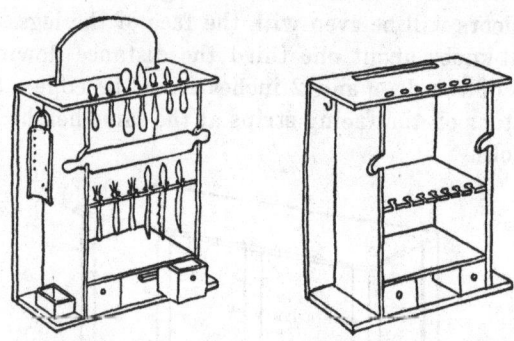

HOUSEWIFE'S HANDY RACK No. 3

Illustration 34 *Figures 1 and 2*

Requirements:

Body. 1 Cereal Box (about 6 in. deep, 17½ in. wide, 23 in. long).

Drawers. 2 Salt Boxes.

Shelves. May be made from the cover removed.

Hardware. 2 very small pull-knobs for drawers. 2 picture hooks and wire.

Construction:

Make the body of the rack the same as described for Small Wall Rack, Illustration No. 21. Fit the shelves. Bore and slot the upper shelf, and bore the holes in the top end, cutting openings for the rolling-pin, the same as described for Housewife's Handy Rack No. 2, Illustration No. 31. The rolling-pin in this rack will hang about midway between the top of the rack and the knife-and-fork shelf.

Remove the covers from the salt boxes and place the boxes in position as shown in the illustration. Fasten with small brads a small guide strip about ¼ inch square along the side and back of each box and to the bottom of the rack, to guide the boxes as well as to prevent them being pushed in too far. Lay the lower shelf on them and fasten it in place with 1½ inch brads driven through the sides and back of the rack into its edges. About midway between this shelf and the top of the rack will be placed the knife-and-fork shelf. Fasten it with brads in the same way. Stand the bread-board across the top of the rack and mark its width near the back on the top of the rack. Measure 2 inches from the back of the rack at these points and bore a 1 inch hole at each point. Connect the edges of these holes with scratch or pencil lines, and with a keyhole-saw cut the slot along the lines for receiving the bread-board. One half of the hole made by the auger will form the end of the slot. The bottom of the bread-board will rest upon the upper shelf. Screw the pull-knobs on the drawers and hang the rack with picture hooks and wire, or screw to the side wall, as may be desired. If to be hung, bore two holes ⅛ inch in diameter through the top, 4 inches from the back and 2 inches from the sides. Pass wire through and knot it on the under side.

CHAPTER VI

LARGER BOXES, APPLYING THE SAME OR SIMILAR
PRINCIPLES AS IN CHAPTER V

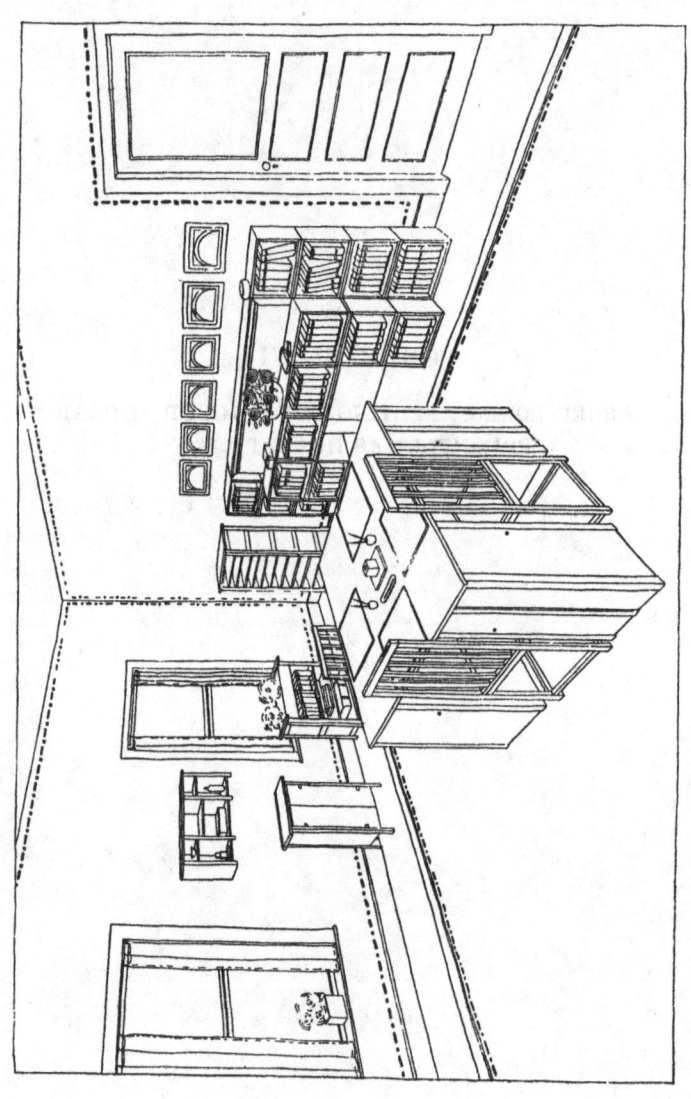

The Office

OFFICE WASHSTAND   FLOWER- AND BOOK-STAND
QUADRUPLE WRITING-DESK
KNICKKNACK BRACKET   OFFICE FILE
FIREPLACE BOOKCASE

The chairs are not made of boxes.

Color Scheme:
    Light oak.
    Tan.
    Olive green.

Woodwork:
    Light oak.

Furniture:
    Light oak.

Walls:
    Burlap in natural color, or with motif stenciled in olive green.

Ceiling:
    Tan in lighter shade than the walls.

Hangings:
    Burlap in olive green.

Curtains:
    Net in same color as hangings.

Floor:
    Stained light oak, with rugs of plain olive green same color as walls.

Plants:
    Growing plants with either crimson or orange-colored blossoms.

CHAPTER VI

Illustration 35

FLOWER-STAND

Box placed top side up; cover removed and used as shelf. Legs added.

Illustration 36

SOILED-LINEN RECEIVER

Box placed top side up; cover removed and hinged as lid. Projecting corner trim and facing strips added.

Illustration 37

SHIRT-WAIST CLOSET

Box placed on end; cover removed and hinged as door. Legs and false top added.

Illustration 38

"NOTIONETTE"

Box placed on end; cover removed and hinged as door. Shelves, corner trim, and false top added.

Illustration 39

OFFICE WASHSTAND

Box placed on end; cover removed and hinged as double door. Shelves, legs, and hinged top added.

Illustration 40

DESK CHAIR

Box placed top side up; cover removed and hinged as lid. Shelf, legs, and arms added.

Illustration 41

QUADRUPLE WRITING-DESK

Eight boxes placed on end. Four have covers removed and hinged as doors. Four have sides removed and hinged as doors. Shelves, corner trims, and false top added.

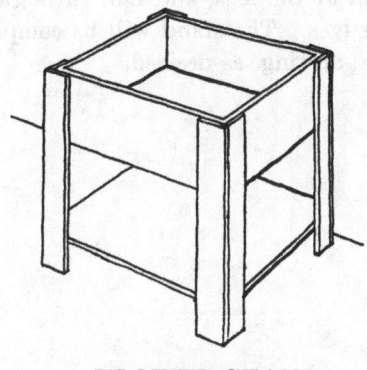

FLOWER-STAND

Illustration 35   *Figure 1*

Requirements:

Body. 1 Candle Box (about 7 in. deep, 12 in. square).

Legs. 4 Strips ⅜ in. thick, 1¼ in. wide, 9 in. longer than the outside depth of the box. 4 Strips ⅜ in. thick, 1½ in. wide, 9 in. longer than the outside depth of the box.

Cleats. 2 Strips ½ in. thick, 1½ in. wide, and length equal to the outside width of the box.

Construction:

Make the legs 9 inches longer than the outside depth of the box. Remove the cover carefully. Nail a cleat across each end on the side presenting the worst appearance, keeping the edge of the cleat even with the end of the cover. Turn the box on its side and nail on the legs, keeping their upper ends even with the top of the box. The cover (with the cleats across the ends to keep it flat) is to be the shelf. Turn the stand upside down and set

92   BOX FURNITURE

the shelf in place between the legs, keeping it 4 inches from the bottom of the legs, and nail through each face of leg into its edges. The stand will be complete, ready for staining or painting, as desired.

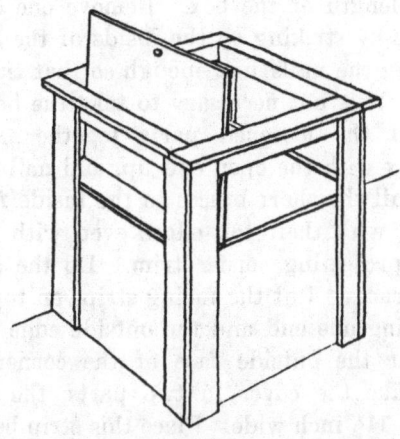

SOILED-LINEN RECEIVER

Illustration 36 *Figure 1*

Requirements:

Body. 1 Tea Box (about 17 in. deep, 17 in. square).

Corner Trim. 4 Strips ½ in. thick, 1½ in. wide, 4 in. longer than the outside length of the box. 4 Strips ½ in. thick, 2 in. wide, 4 in. longer than the outside length of the box.

Braces. 2 Strips ½ in. thick, 1½ in. wide, and length equal to outside depth of the box. 2 Strips ½ in. thick, 1½ in. wide, by 1 in. shorter than the outside width of the box.

Facing Strips. 2 Strips ½ in. thick, 2 in. wide, and length equal to outside depth of the box. 2 Strips ½ in. thick, 2 in. wide, and length equal to outside width of the box.

Cover. 1 Piece ½ in. thick, width equal to the outside depth of the box, and length equal to the outside width of the box.

Hardware. 2 1¾ in. brass hinges (butts) and screws. 1 porcelain pull-knob.

Construction:

Make the projecting corner trim 4 inches longer than the outside length of the box. Remove one end. This may be done by striking on the inside of the box gently and loosening the nails just enough so that they may be drawn out. It is not necessary to take the box entirely apart. Nail the loosened parts together again and stand the box with the open end up, and nail the corner trim on. Nail the short braces to the inside face of the corner trim, with their top edges even with the upper end of the projecting corner trim. Do the same with the longer braces. Put the facing strips on top, flat side down, allowing one end and the outside edge to project ½ inch over the outside face of the corner trim all around. Make the cover in two parts, the rear part being a strip 1½ inch wide. Place this strip between the corner trim on the rear top of the box, with its rear edge against the inner face of the corner trim, and nail both ends and along the back edge. Hang the door to the inner edge of this strip and screw the knob in place.

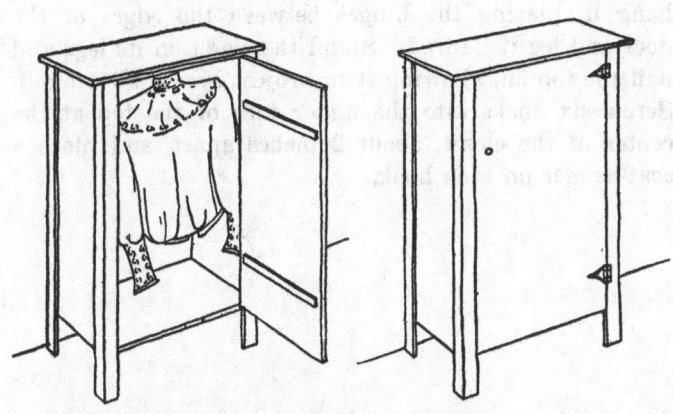

SHIRT-WAIST CLOSET

Illustration 37   *Figures 1 and 2*

Requirements:

Body. 1 Packing Box (about 13 in. deep, 21 in. wide, 33 in. long).

Door. Made from the cover of the box.

Door Cleats. 2 Strips ½ in. thick, 1½ in. wide, 4 in. shorter than the outside width of the box.

Top. 1 Piece ½ in. thick, 3 in. wider and 3 in. longer than the outside width and depth of the box.

Legs. 4 Strips ½ in. thick, 1½ in. wide, 4 in. longer than the outside length of the box. 4 Strips ½ in. thick, 2 in. wide, 4 in. longer than the outside length of the box.

Hardware. 2 1½ in. tee hinges and screws. 1 porcelain pull-knob. 1 brass button and screw. 6 wire hooks. 6 coat-hangers.

Construction:

Make the legs 4 inches longer than the outside length of the box. Remove the cover. Turn the box on its side and nail on the legs. Fit the door, nail the cleats on, and hang it, placing the hinges between the edges of the door and leg if desired. Stand the closet on its legs and nail the top on, allowing it to project evenly all around. Screw six hooks into the under face of the top at the center of the closet, about 2 inches apart, and place a coat-hanger on each hook.

"NOTIONETTE"

Illustration 38 *Figures 1 and 2*

This is a most convenient article where, in a limited space, it is impossible to place a bureau. Two of these were used in a studio for two years, one being used as above and the other as an annex to the desk.

Requirements:

Body. 1 Soap Box (about 8 in. deep, 13¼ in. wide, 27¾ in. long).

Shelves. 5 Pieces ½ in. thick, width equal to the inside depth of the box, and length equal to the inside width of the box.

Shelf Fronts. 5 Pieces ½ in. thick, 2 in. wide, and length equal to the inside width of the box.

Door. Made from the cover of the box.

Cleats. 2 Pieces, ⅜ in. thick, 1½ in. wide, and 4 in. shorter than the outside width of the box.

Corner Trim. 4 Strips ⅜ in. thick, 1⅜ in. wide, and length equal to the outside length of the box. 4 Strips ⅜ in. thick, 1¾ in. wide, and length equal to the outside length of the box.

Top. 1 Piece ½ in. thick, 3 in. wider than the outside depth, and 3 in. longer than the outside width of the box.

Hardware. 2 1¾ in. brass butts and screws. 1 porcelain pull-knob. 1 brass button and screw.

Construction:

Make the corner trim as long as the outside length of the box. Remove the cover, and fit and nail in the shelves at such heights as seem practical, using 1 inch brads driven from outside through into the edge of the shelf. Place a shelf front across the front edge of each shelf, its edge up, and fasten it with brads. Put the corner trim on and nail on the top, allowing it to project evenly all around. Lay the notionette on its back, then put the cleats on the doors and hang them, and screw on the pull-knob and brass button.

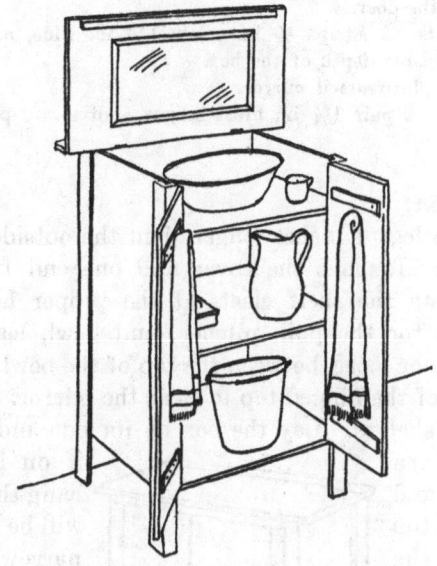

OFFICE WASHSTAND

Illustration 39   *Figures 1 and 2*

Requirements:

Body. 1 Packing Box (about 14 in. deep, 18 in. wide, 36 in. long).

Shelves. 2 Pieces ½ in. thick, width equal to the inside depth of the box, and length equal to the inside width of the box.

Doors. Made from cover of box.

Hinged Top. 1 Piece ½ in. thick, 4 in. wider than the outside depth of the box, and 4 in. longer than the outside width of the box.

Legs. 4 Strips ½ in. thick, 1½ in. wide, and 4 in. longer than the outside length of the box. 4 Strips ½ in. thick, 2 in. wide, and 4 in. longer than the outside length of the box.

BOX FURNITURE

Cleats. 4 Strips ½ in. thick, 1 in. wide, and length equal to the width of the door.

Shelf Cleats. 4 Strips ½ in. thick, 1½ in. wide, and length equal to the inside depth of the box.

Mirror. 1 flat-framed mirror.

Hardware. 1 pair 1¾ in. brass hinges (butts). 2 pairs 4 in. tee hinges.

Construction:

Make the legs 4 inches longer than the outside length of the box. Remove the cover and one end from the box. Put on the shelf cleats at the proper height to make room for the pail, pitcher, and bowl, leaving at least 1 inch, or more, between the top of the bowl and the under side of the hinged top to clear the mirror. Fit and nail in the shelves. Lay the box on its side and put on the legs. Turn it on its back and fit and hang the doors. The hinged top will be made in two pieces, the narrow piece being 6 inches wide. Nail this piece on, letting it project over the face of the legs 1½ inches at the sides and rear. Hang the wide piece of the lid to this, and place a cleat under the front edge to hold the doors closed. Secure the mirror to the under side of the lid.

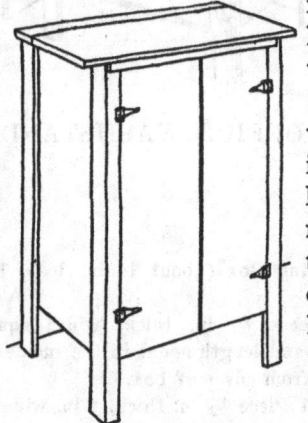

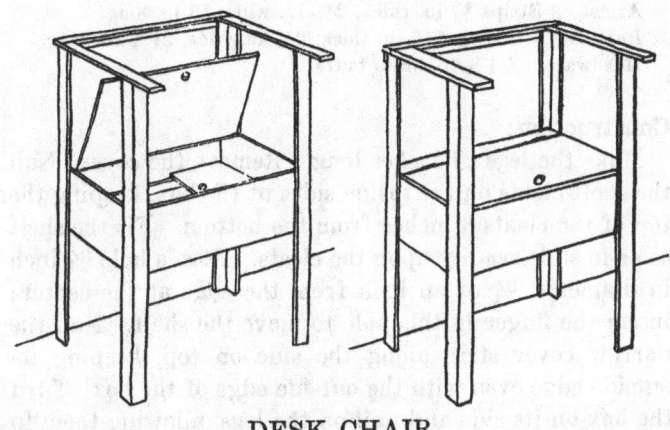

DESK CHAIR

Illustration 40   *Figures 1 and 2*

The seat is formed of a box with a hinged cover. Midway of the depth inside is a sliding shelf upon two cleats extending the length of the box, which provides space for large paper sheets, drawings, etc.

Requirements:

Body. 1 Condensed-milk Box (about 7¼ in. deep, 13 in. wide, 19¾ in. long).

Cover. 1 Piece ⅝ in. thick, 1½ in. wide, length equal to side length of the box. 1 Piece ⅝ in. thick, width 1½ in. less than the width of the box, length equal to the outside length of the box.

Shelf. 1 Piece ½ in. thick, width equal to one-half the inside length of the box, and length equal to the inside width of the box.

Cleats. 2 Pieces ½ in. thick, 1½ in. wide, length equal to the inside length of the box.

Legs. 4 Strips ½ in. thick, 1½ in. wide, 27 in. long. 4 Strips ½ in. thick, 2 in. wide, 27 in. long.

Arms. 2 Strips ½ in. thick, 2½ in. wide, 16 in. long.
Back Bar. 2 Strips ½ in. thick, 2½ in. wide, 21¾ in. long.
Hardware. 2 1¾ in. brass butts.

Construction:

Make the legs 27 inches long. Remove the cover. Nail the shelf cleats on the inside sides of the box, keeping the top of the cleats 3 inches from the bottom. Fit the shelf so as to slide readily upon the cleats. Bore a hole ¾ inch in diameter, ¾ of an inch from the edge at the center; insert the finger in this hole to move the shelf. Nail the narrow cover strip along the side on top, keeping its outside edge even with the outside edge of the box. Turn the box on its side and nail on the legs, allowing them to project 10 inches above the top of the box with the seat cover on. Stand the chair upon its legs, right side up. Nail the arms to the top of the legs, allowing their ends to project 2 inches over the face of the legs in front, and their outside edges to project ½ inch over the outside face of leg on the sides, the rear end of arm being even with the rear face of the rear leg. Nail one of the back bar strips across the rear legs, keeping its top edge even with the top of the leg. Set the other back bar strip, flat side up, directly behind the arm ends, and nail to the other half of back bar already in place. Fit and hang the seat and set the shelf in place.

QUADRUPLE WRITING-DESK

Illustration 41   *Figure 1*

At this desk four persons may work, each having individual narrow and wide closets, with shelves for stationery and book compartments.

Requirements:

Bodies. 8 Soap Boxes (8 in. deep, 13¼ in. wide, 27¾ in. long).

Shelves. 27 Pieces ½ in. thick, length and width equal to the inside width and depth of the box.

Top. 1 Piece ¾ in. thick, 52 in. square (five boards wide).

Tie Strips. 4 Strips ⅝ in. thick, 3 in. wide, 52 in. long.

Corner Trim. 16 Strips ½ in. thick, 1¼ in. wide, length equal to the outside length of the box. 16 Strips ½ in. thick, 1¾ in. wide, length equal to the outside length of the box.

Facing Strips. 8 Strips ½ in. thick, 1¾ in. wide, length equal to the outside length of the box.

Doors. Made from the covers and sides removed.
Door Cleats. 8 Strips ½ in. thick, 1½ in. wide, 10 in. long.
Hardware. 16 1¾ in. hinges (butts) and screws. 8 brass pull-knobs. 8 brass buttons.

Construction:

Make the corner trim as long as the outside length of the box. Remove the covers from four of the boxes and one side from each of the other four boxes. Fit and nail the shelves in the first four boxes, placing the lower one 6 inches from one end of the box. Space the other five evenly between the first shelf and the other end of the box, giving a space of about 3 inches between them. Use 1½ inch brads to fasten the shelves, driving them from the outside through into the edge and ends of the shelves. Fit and nail the shelves in the other four boxes from which the sides were removed, placing the lower shelf 14 inches from one end of the box, and space the other two evenly between this first shelf and the other end of the box.

Place one of the last four boxes bottom down on the floor, with the long compartment at the right-hand end as the open side is faced. Place one of the first four boxes, bottom down (open compartments facing up), upon it, the larger end compartment being at the right-hand end as the open side of the lower box is still faced. Match their edges and nail them together by driving the nails between the shelves, through the bottom of the top box and into the top of the lower box. Use flat-head wire nails, 1¼ inches long, and clinch their points in the lower box. Put the corner trim and the facing strips on. Join the other six boxes together in pairs in the same way. Set each pair of boxes about 20 inches apart, forming a square, all of the closets of a kind at the left hand as you face any side of the square. Miter each end of the four tie strips; lay each one flat side down across two pairs of closets, keeping its ends even with the outside end face of each pair and its outer face even with the front face of each pair, forming a perfect square. Match their mitered ends and nail them to each pair of closets. These strips hold the sets of closets together and the proper distance apart, and upon them is laid the top. Make the top, planing the edges of the boards true and straight. Lay them upon the tie strips. Put hot glue on their edges, and press them tightly together and nail to the tie strips. The top should project 1½ inches over the outer edge of the tie strips on each side. Drive the nail heads slightly below the upper surface of the top and plane smooth the entire top surface of the top.

CHAPTER VII

THE BOX TURNED UPON ITS SIDE, WITH THE COVER AND SOMETIMES THE SIDES REMOVED

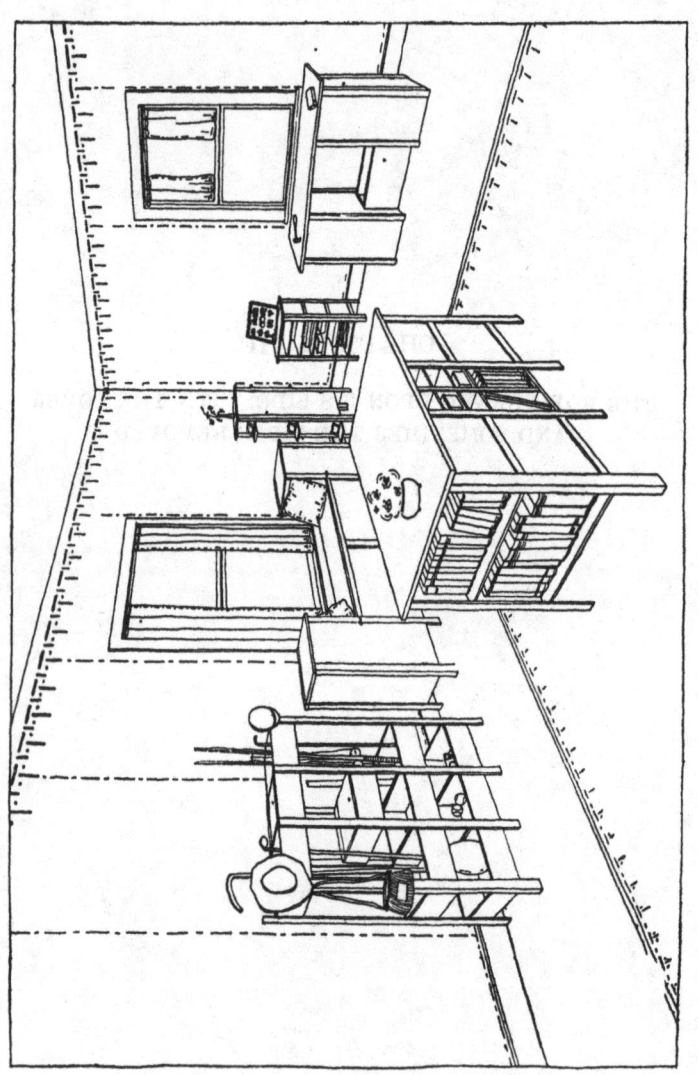

The Boy's Room

BOY'S DELIGHT   PHOTOGRAPHIC-MATERIAL STAND
BOY'S WORK-TABLE
BEDROOM WINDOW-SEAT   MUSIC-STAND
BOY'S BOOK- AND GAME-TABLE

Color Scheme:
  Green.
  Tan.

Woodwork:
  Moss green.

Furniture:
  Moss green.

Walls:
  Tan, with motif stenciled in moss green.

Ceiling:
  Tan.

Hangings and Pillows:
  Tan-colored denim, with motif stenciled in same color as furniture.

Curtains:
  Muslin of tan color, with motif stenciled in same shade as furniture.

Floor:
  Stained same as furniture or color of the walls; rugs olive green with crimson.

Plants:
  Vines and growing plants with either yellow or crimson blossoms.

CHAPTER VII

Illustration 42

FIREPLACE BOOKCASE

Sixteen boxes placed on sides. Four rest upon a frame. Covers removed, otherwise left intact.

Illustration 43

SIMPLE BOOKCASE

Three boxes placed on sides. Covers of all and one side of two removed. Legs and false top added.

Illustration 44

MUSIC-STAND

Three boxes placed top side up. One side of each and covers of two removed. Shelves, legs, and false top added.

Illustration 45

OFFICE FILE

Five boxes placed top side up. One side of each and covers of four removed. Shelves, legs, and false top added.

Illustration 46

500-VOLUME BOOKCASE

Fifteen boxes placed on sides. Covers of all and one side of twelve removed. Corner trim, facing strips, and false top added.

Illustration 47

BOOKCASE WITH DRAWERS

Five boxes placed on sides. Covers of all and one side of four removed. Three smaller boxes used as drawers. Partitions, corner trim, and false top added

Illustration 48

BOY'S BOOK- AND GAME-TABLE

Four boxes placed top side up. Two boxes placed on end. Covers removed. Shelves, legs, and false top added.

Illustration 49

WALL DESK

Box placed on side. Cover removed and hinged as lid. Partition and false top added.

Illustration 50

BOOKCASE DESK

An adaptation of the Wall Desk and the Simple Bookcase in combination.

BOX FURNITURE

FIREPLACE BOOKCASE
Illustration 42 *Figures 1 and 2*

This was set up, inclosing the fireplace just as shown, in a steam-heated studio in the art quarter in New York City and was extremely useful and convenient.

Requirements:
Body. 16 Canned-corn Boxes (about 10¼ in. deep, 11½ in. wide, 15½ in. long).

Bridge Frame. 2 Strips ¾ in. thick, 1½ in. wide, and length equal to four times the outside length of the box. 2 Strips ¾ in. thick, 1½ in. wide, and length 1½ in. shorter than the outside depth of the box with cover removed.

Construction:
Remove the covers from all the boxes. With the strips make a bridge to support the two boxes which are di-

rectly over the fireplace. Place the two long strips on their edge on the floor, and between their ends place the short strips on their edges, and fasten together with two small wire nails driven through the side of the long strips into the ends of the short ones. Place two boxes on their sides, one upon the other, on each side of the fireplace. Lay the frame across these boxes, their outer ends being even with the ends of the frame. Place four boxes upon their sides on the frame. The other two tiers of four boxes each are placed at each end as shown, set back so that their front faces are a little forward of the rear face of the other boxes. Five semicircular photographs of "The Evolution of the Book," by John Alexander, were framed and hung above.

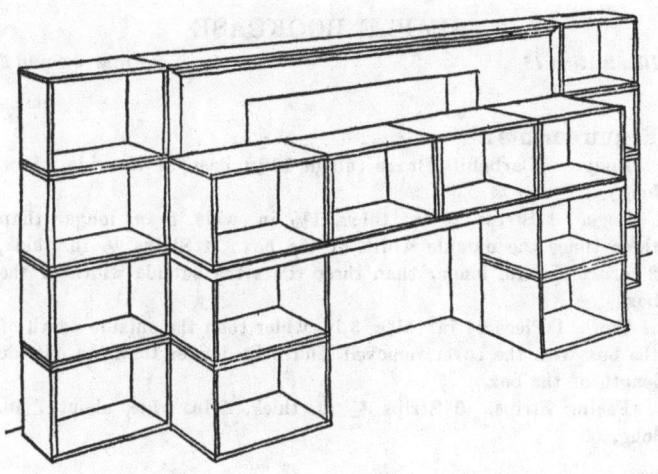

SIMPLE BOOKCASE

Illustration 43   *Figures 1 and 2*

Requirements:

Body. 3 Carbonite Boxes (about 10 in. deep, 12 in. wide, 31 in. long).

Legs. 4 Strips ½ in. thick, 1½ in. wide, 5 in. longer than three times the outside width of the box. 4 Strips ½ in. thick, 2 in. wide, 5 in. longer than three times the outside width of the box.

Top. 1 Piece ⅝ in. thick, 3 in. wider than the outside depth of the box with the cover removed, and 3 in. longer than the outside length of the box.

Facing Strips. 6 Strips ½ in. thick, 2 in. wide, about 7 in. long.

Construction:

Make the legs 5 inches longer than three times the outside width of the box. Remove the covers. Turn one box on its side and remove the upper side. Do the same with the second box. Place the second box on its side upon the open side of the first box, keeping the open side of the second box at the top. Upon this open side of the second box place the third box, keeping all the cover openings facing the same way. Fasten the three boxes together by nailing two strips placed vertically across the bottoms about 2 feet apart, to hold them together while the legs are put on. Turn all three boxes on their backs and nail on the legs, keeping their upper ends even with the top side of the last box added. Turn the stand upon its legs and nail on the top, allowing its edges to project 1 inch over the outside face of the legs all around. Put on the facing strips at the ends and remove the temporary strips from the back of the stand.

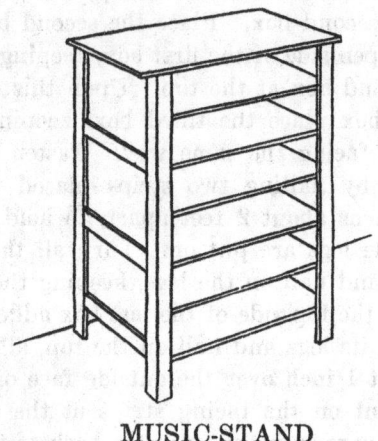

MUSIC-STAND

Illustration 44 *Figure 1*

Requirements:

Body. 3 Condensed-milk Boxes (about 7¼ in. deep, 13 in. wide, 19¾ in. long).

Shelves. 3 Pieces ½ in. thick, by the inside width and length of the box.

Top. 1 Piece ½ in. thick, 2½ in. wider and 3 in. longer than the outside width and length of the box.

Legs. 4 Strips ½ in. thick, 1¼ in. wide, 27 in. long. 4 Strips ½ in. thick, 1¾ in. wide, 27 in. long.

Facing Strips. 6 Strips ½ in. thick, 1¾ in. wide, about 10 in. long. Use the covers and sides removed in making the shelves.

Construction:

Make the legs 27 inches long. Remove the covers from two of the boxes. Turn one box on its side and remove the upper side. Do the same with the second and third boxes. Place the second box, bottom down, upon the open top of the first box, keeping the open top of the second box facing up. Upon this open top of the second box place the third box, keeping all the open sides facing the same way. Fasten the three boxes together by nailing two strips placed vertically across the rear sides, about 15 inches apart, to hold them together while the legs are put on. Turn all three boxes on their reverse sides and nail on the legs, keeping their upper ends even with the top of the last box added. Turn the stand upon its legs and nail on the top, allowing its edges to project 1 inch over the outside face of the legs all around. Put the facing strips on the ends of the stand and remove the temporary strips from the back. Fit the shelves in place, one in the lower, one in the middle, and one in the top compartment, using care to have them equal heights at the ends, so they will all be parallel. Fasten the shelves in place with 1½ inch brads driven from the outside, through the ends of the stand, into the ends of the shelves.

NOTE. If two shelves, instead of one, are placed in each of the upper boxes, as shown in the Boy's Room Interior, sheet music can be held more conveniently than if made as herein described.

BOX FURNITURE

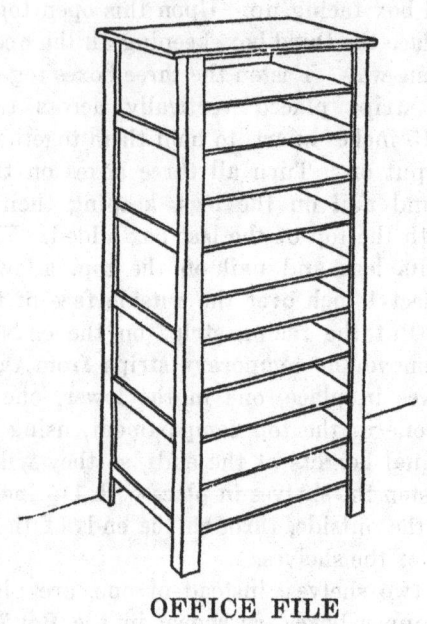

OFFICE FILE
Illustration 45 *Figure 1*

Requirements:

Body. 5 Condensed-milk Boxes (about 7¼ in. deep, 13 in. wide, 19¾ in. long).

Shelves. 5 Pieces ½ in. thick, by the inside width and length of the box.

Top. 1 Piece ½ in. thick, 3 in. wider and 3 in. longer than the outside width and length of the box.

Legs. 4 Strips ½ in. thick, 1¼ in. wide, 38 in. long. 4 Strips ½ in. thick, 1¾ in. wide, 38 in. long.

Facing Strips. 10 Strips ½ in. thick, 1¾ in. wide, about 10 in. long. Use the covers and sides removed, in making the shelves.

Construction:

Make the legs 38 inches long. Remove the covers from four of the boxes. Turn one box on its side and remove its upper side. Do the same with the second, third, fourth, and fifth boxes. Place the second box, bottom down, upon the open top of the first box, keeping the open top of the second box facing up, and place the third upon the second, and the fourth upon the third, and the fifth upon the fourth, in like manner, keeping all the open sides facing the same way. Fasten the five boxes together by nailing two strips placed vertically across the rear sides about 15 inches apart to hold them together while the legs are put on. Turn all five boxes on their reverse sides and nail on the legs, keeping their upper ends even with the top of the last box added. Turn the stand upon its legs and nail on the top, allowing its edges to project 1 inch over the outside face of the legs all around. Put the facing strips on the ends of the stand and remove the temporary strips from the back.

NOTE. If two shelves, instead of one, are placed in each of the two upper boxes, as shown in the Office Interior, sheet stationery, in a limited quantity, can be more conveniently accommodated than if made as herein described.

500-VOLUME BOOKCASE

Illustration 46 *Figure 1*

Made from fifteen silk boxes, with their covers removed, twelve of them having also one side removed. Provides space for five hundred volumes.

Requirements:

Body. 15 Silk Boxes (about 7½ in. deep, 7½ in. wide, 35 in. long).

Top. 1 Piece ⅝ in. thick, 2 in. wider than the outside depth of the box with the cover removed, and 9 in. longer than the box. 1 Piece ⅝ in. thick, 2 in. wider than the outside depth of the box with the cover removed, and 9 in. longer than twice the length of the box.

Facing Strips. 3 Strips ½ in. thick, 2 in. wide, and length equal to about five times the width of the box. 10 Strips ½ in. thick, 2 in. wide, and length about 3 in. shorter than the depth of the box.

Corner Trim. 7 Strips ½ in. thick, 1½ in. wide, and length equal to about five times the width of the box. 7 Strips ½ in. thick, 2 in. wide, and length equal to about five times the width of the box.

Construction:

Make the corner trim about five times longer than the width of the box. Remove the covers from all the boxes and also one side from twelve of them. Place on their sides one upon the other, each with its open side up, four of the boxes from which both a cover and one side have been removed, and upon these four place one also on its side from which the cover only has been removed, keeping the top or cover openings all facing the same way. Fasten the five boxes together by, first, putting the rear corner trim at each end, then the front corner trim at one end only. As the other end is to connect with the other two sections of the rack, the corner trim at that end will be put on the reverse way after the sections are ready to join together. Therefore a facing strip will be placed on the end face of each section at the corner end. The front edge of the facing strip is to be placed even with the front edge of the rack and nailed to the ends of the boxes.

The double section of the rack is built up in the same manner as the single section just described. The ends of the two sections forming the double section are placed against each other and joined by nailing together, a facing strip being placed over the joint in both front and rear, two pieces of corner trim at the outer end and one piece of corner trim and a facing strip at the inner or corner end, the same as that of the single section. Place the two sections at right angles to each other and bring the front face corners together. Set the corner trim the reverse way in the angle and nail it to the front faces of both sections to join and hold the sections together. Put the short facing strips on the outer ends and fit and nail

122   BOX FURNITURE

the top on, keeping its rear edge even with the outer face of the trim and allowing its ends and front edge to project 1 inch over the front face of the trim, with a miter-joint at the corner.

BOOKCASE WITH DRAWERS
Illustration 47   *Figure 1*

Requirements:
Body. 5 Umbrella Boxes (10 in. square, 44 in. long).

Drawers. 1 Box (about 9 in. deep, 9½ in. wide, 17½ in. long). 2 Boxes (about 9 in. deep, 9½ in. wide, 12 in. long).

Corner Trim. 4 Strips ½ in. thick, 1½ in. wide, length equal to five times the outside width of the box. 4 Strips ½ in. thick, 2 in. wide, and length equal to five times the outside width of the box.

Top. 1 Piece ⅝ in. thick, 3 in. wider than the outside depth of the box with the cover removed, 3 in. longer than the outside length of the box.

Partition. 2 Pieces ½ in. thick, width equal to the inside depth of the box, and length equal to the inside width of the box.

Facing Strips. 10 Strips ½ in. thick, 2 in. wide, about 7 in. long.

Hardware. 3 drawer pulls.

Construction:
Make the corner trim five times the outside width of the box. Remove the covers. Turn one large box on its

side and remove the upper side. Do the same with the second, third, and fourth large boxes. Place the second box on its side upon the open side of the first box, keeping the open side of the second box at the top, and place the third upon the second, and the fourth upon the third, in like manner. Upon the open side of the fourth box place the fifth box on its side without having removed either side, keeping all the cover or top openings facing the same way. Fasten the five boxes together by nailing two strips placed vertically across the bottoms about 2 feet apart, to hold them together while the corner trim is put on. Turn all five boxes on the reverse side and nail on the corner trim, keeping their upper ends even with the top side of the last box added. Turn the stand right side up and nail on the top, allowing its edges to project 1 inch over the outside face of the trim all around. Place the two smallest boxes in the lower compartment, one at each end, and set the partitions in place, one against the side of each drawer, and nail them fast. Fit in the middle drawer and fasten the drawer pulls on. Put on the facing strips at the ends and remove the temporary strips from the back.

NOTE. In the illustration one drawer is removed, showing a strip against the end, the thickness of the corner trim projection over the face of the compartment, which acts as a guide for the drawer. It is the same at each end of the stand.

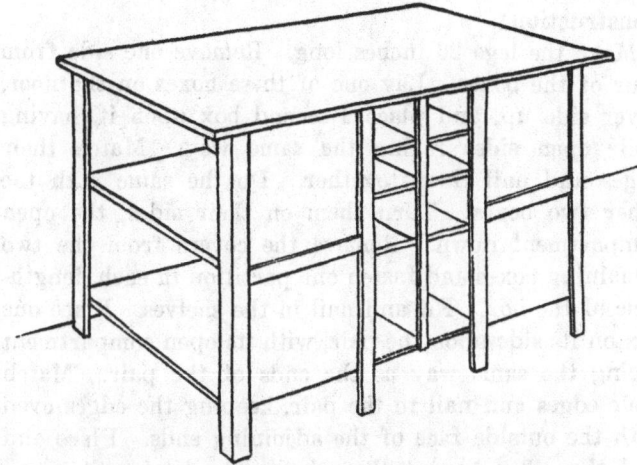

BOY'S BOOK- AND GAME-TABLE
Illustration 48 *Figure 1*

Requirements:

Body. 6 Starch Boxes (about 10⅞ in. deep, 13⅛ in. wide, 22 in. long).

Top. 1 Piece ½ in. thick, 6 in. wider than the outside length of the box, and 6 in. longer than three times the outside width of the box.

Shelves. 12 Pieces ⅜ in. thick, width ⅜ in. less than one half the inside width of the box, and length equal to the inside depth of the box.

Partitions. 2 Pieces ⅜ in. thick, width equal to the inside depth of the box, and length equal to the inside length of the box.

Legs. 4 Strips ⅜ in. thick, 1⅜ in. wide, 26 in. long. 4 Strips ⅜ in. thick, 1¾ in. wide, 26 in. long.

Facing Strip Legs. 4 Strips ⅜ in. thick, 1¾ in. wide, 26 in. long.

Horizontal Facing Strips. 2 Strips ⅜ in. thick, 1¾ in. wide, and 1⅞ in. shorter than the outside length of the box.

Construction:

Make the legs 26 inches long. Remove one side from four of the boxes. Lay one of these boxes on the floor, cover side up, and place a second box upon it, having their open sides facing the same way. Match their edges and nail them together. Do the same with the other two boxes. Turn them on their sides, the open compartment down. Remove the covers from the two remaining boxes and fasten one partition in each, lengthwise of the box. Fit and nail in the shelves. Place one box on its side upon the pair, with its open compartment facing the same way as the ends of the pair. Match their edges and nail to the pair, keeping the edges even with the outside face of the adjoining ends. Place and nail the other box at the other ends, having its open compartment facing the same way as the other ends of the pair, or directly opposite that of the other box having shelves. There will be a small space between the side compartment boxes which will be hidden by the top. Upon the last two boxes place the other pair, with their open sides facing up, and nail them to the others. Nail on the legs, also the facing strip legs, allowing their inner edges to project $\frac{1}{2}$ inch over the inner side faces of the shelved compartments. Nail on the horizontal facing strips between the facing strip legs and the corner legs. Each end of the table has two open compartments. Both sides are also alike, each having a shelved compartment as shown. Fit and nail on the top, allowing an even projection of $2\frac{5}{8}$ inches over the outside face of the leg on all sides.

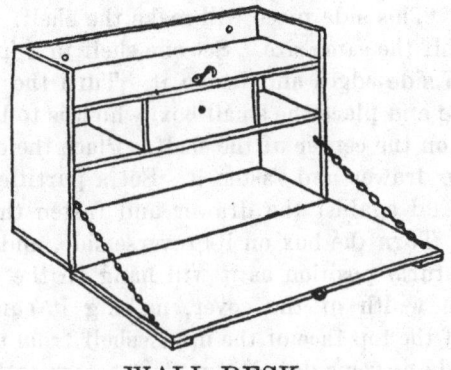

WALL DESK

Illustration 49 *Figure 1*

Requirements:

Body. 1 Box (about 8¾ in. deep, 15¾ in. wide, 30 in. long).

Drawer. 1 Five-pound Candy Box (about 3½ in. deep, 7 in. wide, 13 in. long).

Shelves. 2 Pieces ½ in. thick. One may be made from the side removed.

Partition. 2 Pieces ½ in. thick, width equal to the depth of the drawer, length equal to the inside depth of the box.

Lid. Made from the cover.

Cleats. 2 Pieces ½ in. thick, 1½ in. wide, length equal to the width of the lid.

Hardware. 2 Pieces of brass sash chain, each about 10 in. long. 4 brass screws ½ in. long. 2 1¾ in. butts and screws. 1 small brass hook and screw-eye. 1 small brass pull-knob.

Construction:

Remove the cover and one side. Cut off the ends of the side which has been removed to make its length the same as the inside length of the box. Plane one side edge to make its width the same as the inside depth of the box. This side piece will make the shelf. Make another shelf the same size. Set one shelf in 2 inches from the open side edges and fasten it. Turn the box on its open side and place the small box, which is to become the drawer, on the center of the shelf. Place the other shelf upon the drawer and fasten it. Set a partition on each side of and against the drawer and fasten them to the shelves. Turn the box on its reverse side, and it will be in its natural position as it will hang on the wall. Reduce the width of the cover, making it equal to the height of the top face of the upper shelf from the bottom face of the lower side. Put a cleat across each end and the full width of the lid, keeping its edge even with the end, and hang it, placing the hinges on the edge faces. The top edge of the lid when the desk is closed should be even with the upper side of the top shelf. Fasten the chains by a screw (passed through a link at one end), secured to the inside face of the top of the desk. The other end of the chain is to be fastened in a similar manner to the lid ¾ inch from the side edge and 4 inches from the top edge of the lid, the cleats being on the outside face. Screw the pull-knob to the center of the face of the drawer.

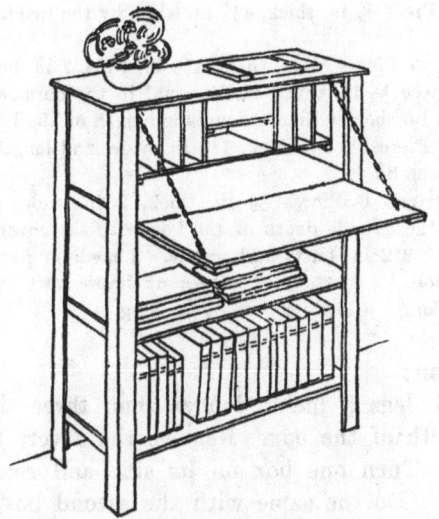

BOOKCASE DESK

Illustration 50   *Figures 1 and 2*

Made from three carbonite boxes and one cigar box. Space for books, magazines, writing equipment, and desk.

Requirements:

Body. 3 Carbonite Boxes (about 10 in. deep, 12 in. wide, 31 in. long). 1 Cigar Box.

Legs. 4 Pieces ½ in. thick, 1½ in. wide, 5 in. longer than three times the outside width of the box. 4 Pieces ½ in. thick, 2 in. wide, 5 in. longer than three times the outside width of the box.

Top. 1 Piece ⅝ in. thick, 3 in. wider than the outside depth of the box with cover removed, 3 in. longer than the outside length of the box.

Shelf. 1 Piece ⅜ in. thick, 4½ in. wide, by the inside length of the box.

Partition. 7 Pieces ⅜ in. thick, 4½ in. wide, 7 in. long.

Lid. 1 Piece ½ in. thick, width equal to the outside width of the box, by 3 in. shorter than the outside length of the box.

Cleats. 2 Pieces ½ in. thick, 1½ in. wide, and length equal to the width of the lid.

Facing Strips. 6 Pieces ½ in. thick, 2 in. wide, and 3 in. shorter than the outside depth of the box with the cover removed.

Hardware. 2 2 in. butts and screws. 1 medium pull-knob. 1 small pull-knob. 1 button. 2 pieces of brass sash chain, each about 10 in. long. 4 brass screws ½ in. long.

Construction:

Make the legs 5 inches longer than three times the outside width of the box. Remove the covers from all the boxes. Turn one box on its side and remove the upper side. Do the same with the second box. Place the second box on its side upon the open side of the first box, keeping the open side of the second box at the top. Upon this open side of the second box place the third box, keeping all the openings facing the same way. Fasten the three boxes together by nailing two strips placed vertically across the bottoms about 2 feet apart to hold them together while the legs are put on. Turn all three boxes on the reverse side and nail on the legs, keeping their upper ends even with the top of the last box added. Turn the stand upon its legs and nail on the top, allowing its edges to project 1 inch over the outside face of the legs all around. Remove the temporary strips from the back. Cut and nail the facing strips on each end, keeping the bottom edge of the lower ones even with the under side of the body.

Fit and nail in the shelf, keeping 7 inches height of

BOX FURNITURE 131

space above it. Set the cigar box at the center of the shelf and place and nail the partitions which are to support it, then place and nail the short shelf, using small brads. Place the other partitions at such places as will be most convenient.

Put a cleat across each end and the full width of the lid, keeping its edge even with the end of the lid. Fit the lid in place and hang it, and screw on the pull-knob and the button.

Fasten the chains with a screw (passed through a link at one end) to the inside face of the top, about 1 inch from the end. The other end of the chain is to be fastened in a similar manner to the lid.

CHAPTER VIII

ONE OR MORE BOXES SUPPORTED ONE ABOVE THE OTHER BY EITHER CORNER TRIM OR LEGS

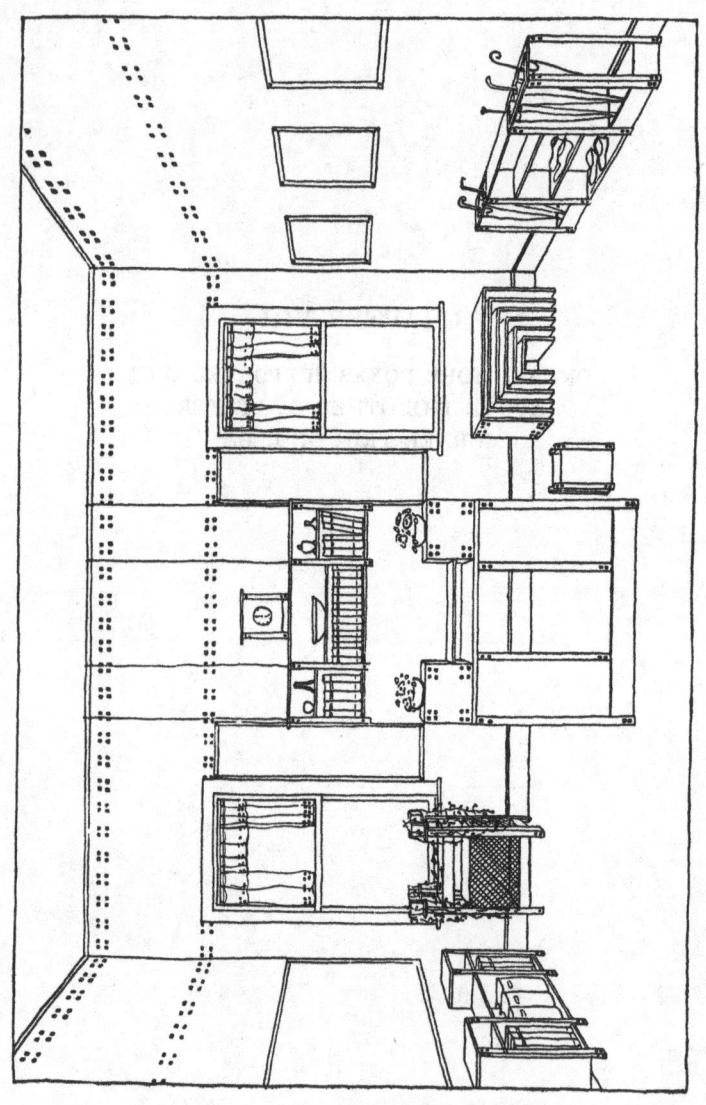

The School-room

REFERENCE STAND

NATURE-STUDY STAND   TEACHER'S DESK

UPRIGHT CLOCK

BOOK AND KNICKKNACK BRACKET   SCRAP-BOX

NEST OF BENCHES

UMBRELLA- AND OVERSHOE-STAND

Color Scheme:
  Dark oak.
  Light brown.

Woodwork:
  Dark oak.

Furniture:
  Dark oak, with motif stenciled in same color as walls.

Walls:
  Light brown, with motif stenciled in same color as woodwork.

Ceiling:
  Same color as walls, but lighter shade.

Curtains:
  Unbleached cotton cloth, and motif stenciled with the light and dark browns used on the walls and woodwork.

Floor:
  Stained dark brown and finished with shellac.

Plants:
  Evergreens, growing vines, plants, and cut flowers of one color or varying hues of same; for instance, a harmony of cream or orange or red.

CHAPTER VIII

Illustration 51
ODDS-AND-ENDS STAND
Three plant-boxes in combination. Legs added.

Illustration 52
ROLLING SOILED-DISH STAND
Two boxes placed top side up. Covers removed. Corner trim, casters, and removable false top added.

Illustration 53
FLOWER- AND BOOK-STAND
Two boxes placed on sides. Covers removed. Shelf, side strips, and legs added.

Illustration 54
BEDSIDE STAND
Similar to Flower- and Book-Stand. Doors and false top added.

Illustration 55
"SILVERETTE"
Four boxes placed top side up. Covers removed. Three covers hinged as lids. Partitions, legs, and false top added.

Illustration 56
GAME-TABLE
Two boxes placed on end. Covers and bottoms removed. Shelves, legs, and false top added.

Illustration 57
TWIN-BED NIGHT TABLE
Two boxes placed top side up. One has side removed and hinged as door. One has both ends removed. Partition, legs, and false top added.

Illustration 58
NATURE-STUDY STAND
Two boxes placed top side up. Four boxes placed top side up. Covers of all removed. Legs and wire netting added.

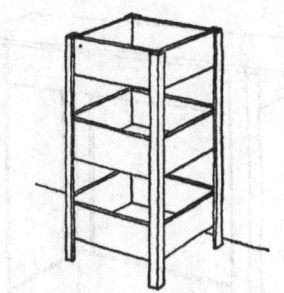

ODDS-AND-ENDS STAND

Illustration 51 *Figure 1*

Requirements:

Body. 3 Bottled-bean Boxes (about 7¾ in. deep, 11¾ in. wide, 12¼ in. long).

Legs. 4 Strips ⅜ in. thick, 1⅛ in. wide, 36 in. long. 4 Strips ⅜ in. thick, 1½ in. wide, 36 in. long.

Construction:

Make the legs 36 inches long. Remove the covers. Turn one box on its side and nail on two of the legs, allowing one end of each to project 4 inches from the bottom face of the box. Place the second box on its side, with its open top facing in the same direction as the open top of the first box, and nail the other end of the legs to it, keeping their ends even with the open-top edges of the box. Set the third box between the two end boxes, evenly spaced, and nail the legs to it. Turn the three boxes upside down and nail the other legs on in the same manner.

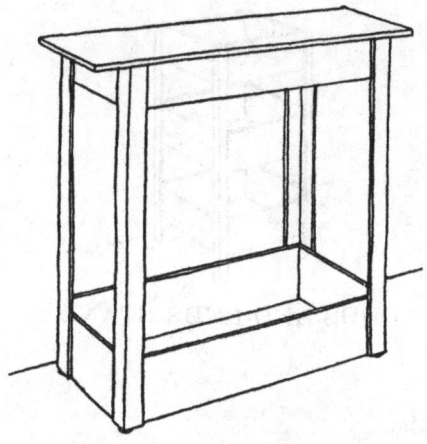

ROLLING SOILED-DISH STAND

Illustration 52 *Figures 1 and 2*

This stand is intended to convey the soiled dishes from the dining-room to the kitchen.

Requirements:
Body. 2 Picture Boxes (about 5½ in. deep, 18 in. wide, 30 in. long).
Top. 1 Piece ½ in. thick, 3 in. wider and 4 in. longer than the outside size of the box.
Legs. 4 Strips ⅝ in. thick, 1⅝ in. wide, 27 in. long. 4 Strips ⅝ in. thick, 2¼ in. wide, 27 in. long.
Hardware. 4 casters and screws.

Construction:
Make the legs 27 inches long. Remove the covers. Turn one box on its side and nail on two of the legs.

Keep the ends of the legs even with the bottom of the box. Nail the other ends of the legs to the other box, keeping the open top of both boxes facing the same way and the ends of the legs even with the top of the box. Turn both boxes on the other side and nail the other two legs in the same way to both boxes. Turn both boxes so the legs will stand in a vertical position, with the top of the last box resting flat on the floor. Place and fasten a caster with screws under each corner of the bottom compartment. Nail a cleat, 1½ inches wide and 5 inches shorter than the width of the top, on the under side of the top, 5 inches from each end. The top will not be nailed, as it is to be used as a cover or loose top.

NOTE. The Smoker's Table shown in the Den Interior is made in the same manner as the Rolling Soiled-dish Stand, but from smaller boxes.

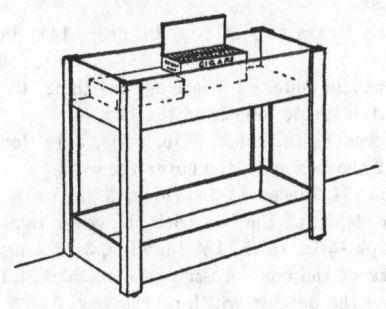

FLOWER- AND BOOK-STAND
Illustration 53   *Figures 1 and 2*

Requirements:

Body. 2 Soap Boxes (about 10¾ in. deep, 14¼ in. wide, 20 in. long).

Flower Receptacle Side. 1 Piece ½ in. thick, 6 in. wide, and length equal to the inside length of the box.

Arms. 2 Pieces ½ in. thick, 3 in. wide, 3 in. longer than the outside depth of the box with the cover removed.

Facing Strips. 4 Pieces ½ in. thick, 3 in. wide, 3 in. shorter than the outside depth of the box with the cover removed.

Legs. 4 Strips ½ in. thick, 1½ in. wide, 3 in. longer than twice the outside width of the box. 4 Strips ½ in. thick, 2 in. wide, 3 in. longer than twice the outside width of the box.

Cleats. 4 Strips ½ in. thick, 2 in. wide, and length equal to the inside depth of the box.

Construction:

Make the legs 3 inches longer than twice the outside width of the box. Remove the covers. Take one box.

BOX FURNITURE 141

which will form the two lower compartments. Turn it on its side; remove the top side; cut the side removed to the inside length and width of the box. Set it in halfway down to form the shelf, having previously nailed a cleat on each end to support it. Take the other box and turn it upon its side and remove the top side. Across each inside end of the box nail a cleat. Keep the top of the cleat 6 inches below the top of the ends to support the bottom of the flower receptacle. Set both boxes on the floor, side by side, on their original bottoms, and hold them close together while the legs are nailed in place. Keep their top ends even with the edges of the open side of the box which will form the flower receptacle. Fit the front side of the flower receptacle and nail it to the inside face of the legs. Turn the stand right side up on its legs. From the spare side removed from the box, cut and fit the bottom of the flower receptacle and nail it to the cleats. At each end of the stand cover the joint midway the height with a facing strip placed centrally over the joint and nailed to the ends of both boxes. Nail another facing strip at each lower end of the stand, keeping the bottom of the strip even with the under side of the arms, the stand. Set the arms, giving them a projection over the legs of 1 inch at the ends and side. Nail the shelf in lower compartment to the cleats, and stain or paint as may be desired.

BOX FURNITURE

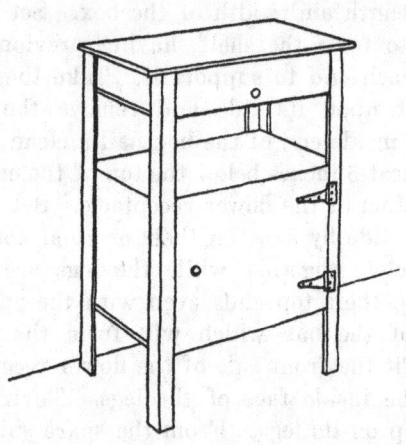

BEDSIDE STAND

Illustration 54   *Figure 1*

Requirements:

Body. 1 Soap Box (about 10¾ in. deep, 14¼ in. wide, 20 in. long). 1 Box (about 5 in. deep, 14¼ in. wide, 20 in. long).

Upper Door. 1 Piece ½ in. thick, 6 in. wide, 3 in. shorter than the length of the outside of the box.

Top. 1 Piece ½ in. thick, 1½ in. wider than the outside depth of the box, 3 in. longer than the outside length of the box.

Door Cleats. 2 Pieces ½ in. thick, 2 in. wide, 4 in. shorter than the outside width of the box.

Legs. 4 Pieces ½ in. thick, 1½ in. wide, 30 in. long. 4 Pieces ½ in. thick, 2 in. wide, 30 in. long.

Hardware. 2 pull-knobs. 2 3 in. tee hinges and screws. 2 1½ in. butts and screws.

Lower Door. The lower door is to be made from the cover removed from the box.

Construction:

Make the legs 30 inches long. Remove the cover from the larger box. Nail a leg to each corner of this box, allowing the ends to project exactly 6 inches on one side. Turn in an upright position upon its legs.

Remove one side from the smaller box and nail the cover down level and securely. Set this box between the long projecting ends of the legs, keeping its top even with the top ends of the legs, and nail the legs to it. Have the open sides of the boxes facing the same way. Place the top in position, keeping the rear edge even with the face of the legs and projecting evenly at the front and ends, and drive the nails near the edges and into the sides of the box, so they will not be exposed either inside or outside.

Make the doors. The face of each door is to be even with the face of the legs. The length of the doors will be the distance between the legs, and the depth will be the outside depth of the box. Hang the upper door from its top by the 1½ inch butts, one half of the butt being secured to the face of the door and the other half to the under side projecting edge of the top. Put the cleats on the lower door and hang with the tee hinges screwed to the face of both legs and door. Place pull-knob on upper door 1½ inches and on lower door 2½ inches from the edge of the door. Small spring catches or buttons may be placed on the doors if desired to hold them closed.

BOX FURNITURE

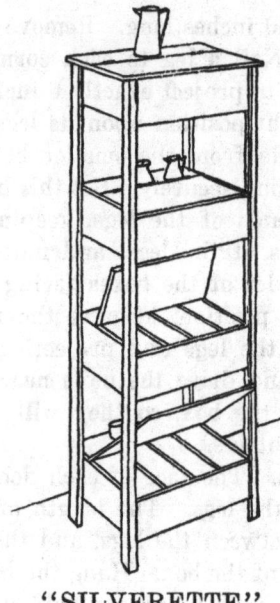

"SILVERETTE"

Illustration 55   *Figure 1*

This piece was used in a limited space for one year in a model flat in a tenement district and one year in a studio in the art quarter.

Requirements:
Body. 4 Bottled Soda Water Boxes (about 15 in. wide, 20 in. long, 4 in. deep).

Cover. 3 Covers made from the box tops. 1 Cover 3 in. wider and 3 in. longer than the boxes.

Partitions. 9 Pieces ½ in. thick, width equal to the inside depth of the boxes, length equal to the inside width of the boxes.

Legs. 4 Strips ½ in. thick, 1½ in. wide, 56 in. long. 4 Strips ½ in. thick, 2 in. wide, 56 in. long.

Hardware. 8 1½ in. hinges (butts) and screws.

Construction:

Make the legs 56 inches long. Remove the covers. Fit and nail the partitions in the boxes, spacing them to suit the various articles they will contain. The top box is to be used as one compartment for table linen.

Fasten the partitions in place with 1¼ inch brads driven from the outside of the box into the ends and lower edges of the partitions. The covers will be in two parts hinged together, the rear part, 4 inches wide, to be nailed on the rear top part of the box, with its back edge even with the outside face of the rear side of the box. Hang the wide portion of the cover to this narrow portion with the butts or hinges. The cover of the top box will be 3 inches wider and longer than the other three, as it will project 1½ inches over the outside face of the box all around. The narrow portion of this cover will be 5½ inches wide. Having hung all the covers on the boxes, place them in a row upon the floor, rear side up, with all the covers facing the same way, keeping a space of about 11 inches between them. Nail the rear legs to the bottom box, allowing the leg to project 6 inches below the bottom. Set the top box so that the upper ends of the legs will come even with the under side of the cover. Nail the legs to this box also. Move the two intermediate boxes until the spaces between all the boxes are the same. Nail the legs to the intermediate boxes. Turn the four boxes completely, so that they will face front side up, and adjust and nail on the other legs in the same manner. Stand the "silverette" on its legs.

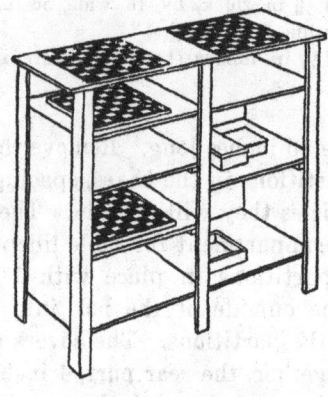

GAME-TABLE

Illustration 56 *Figures 1, 2, and 3*

This table, made by the writer as herein described, has been in daily use at the Copenhagen Settlement in Denmark for more than a year. The checkers used were sawed from broom handles, one half of which were stained black, making 30 checkers in all.

Requirements:

Body. 2 Butter Boxes (15 in. deep, 15 in. wide, 20 in. long).

Top. 1 Piece ½ in. thick, 3 in. wider than the depth of the box with the cover and bottom removed, 3 in. longer than twice the outside width of the box.

Legs. 4 Strips ½ in. thick, 1½ in. wide, 9½ in. longer than the outside length of the box. 4 Strips ½ in. thick, 2 in. wide, 9½ in. longer than outside length of the box.

Facing Strips. 2 Strips ½ in. thick, 2 in. wide, 9½ in. longer than the outside length of the box.

Shelves. The shelves can be made from the covers and bottoms removed.

End Cleats. 2 Strips ½ in. thick, 1½ in. wide, and length 3 in. shorter than the width of the top.

Middle Cleats. 1 Strip ½ in. thick, 2 in. wide, and length 3 in. shorter than the width of the top.

Construction:

Make the legs 9½ inches longer than the outside length of the box. Remove the cover and bottom from each box. Draw lines across the inside face of the sides of the boxes where the shelves are to be placed. In one box they will be located, one shelf one third and the

other shelf two thirds the height of the box. In the other box the shelf will be one half the height. Fit the shelves and fasten them with 1¼ inch brads driven from the outside through the sides of the box into the edges of the shelves. Having put the shelves in both, lay one box upon its side and place the other box, upon its side, upon the first box. Match their edges and nail them together. Now put on the legs and facing strips which also act as intermediate legs, using care that all the legs project 4 inches at their lower ends and 5½ inches at their upper ends, then stand the table upon its legs.

Set the cover on the legs, keeping an even projection all around, and drive three nails through the top into the upper end of each corner leg and two nails into the intermediate legs. The nails should be 2 inches long to hold well. On the top, directly over the center of each compartment, draw a 12 inch square and divide each side of the square into eight equal spaces, then draw parallel lines across both ways, thus dividing the large square into 64 small squares. Sandpaper the top face and whiten it, then blacken in every other square and give the whole top face a coat of varnish. The balance of the table can be stained or painted any desired color.

NOTE. The Toy Cupboard shown in the Nursery Interior is one section of the Game-table made without the top skeleton compartment and with four legs, and placed at each end of the Shoe Cupboard, which is made without either corner trim or corner legs.

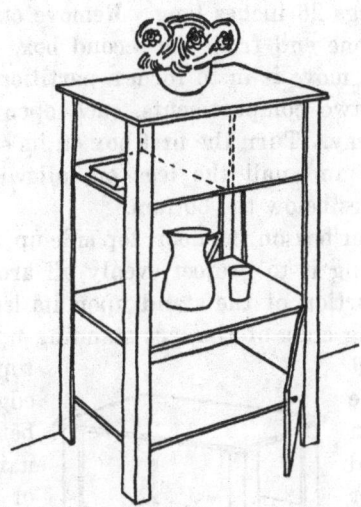

TWIN-BED NIGHT TABLE

Illustration 57   *Figures 1 and 2*

Made of two boxes. Space for water-pitcher, glasses, books, and night conveniences.

Requirements:

Body. 2 Cleanser Boxes (about 9¼ in. deep, 13¾ in. wide, 20 in. long).

Legs. 4 Strips ½ in. thick, 1¼ in. wide, 26 in. long. 4 Strips ½ in. thick, 1¾ in. wide, 26 in. long.

Door. Made from the side of the box.

Top. 1 Piece ½ in. thick, 3 in. wider than the outside width of the box, 3 in. longer than the outside length of the box.

Hardware. 2 1¾ in. butts and screws. 1 brass pull-knob. 1 brass button.

Construction:

Make the legs 26 inches long. Remove one side from one box and one end from the second box. Loosen the other end and move it in to form a partition in the center, forming two compartments, each open end facing the opposite way. Turn the first box on its side with the open side up and nail the legs on, allowing them to project 3 inches below the bottom.

Lay the other box on the floor, top side up, and nail the top on, allowing it to project evenly all around. Turn the bottom portion of the stand upon its legs, with the long projecting ends of the legs standing up, then raise the completed top compartment by the edges of its top, and set it in between all four legs and nail the legs to each corner of it.

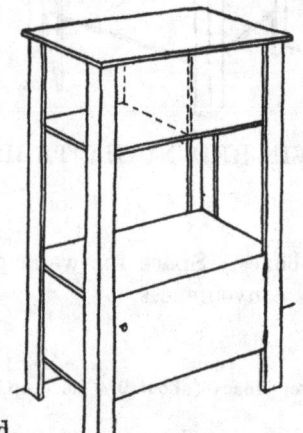

Fit and hang the door, and screw on the pull-knob and brass button to hold the door closed. The upper compartment is closed on the sides and open at both ends and has a partition in the center.

The lower compartment has only the door opening. The rest is closed.

BOX FURNITURE 151

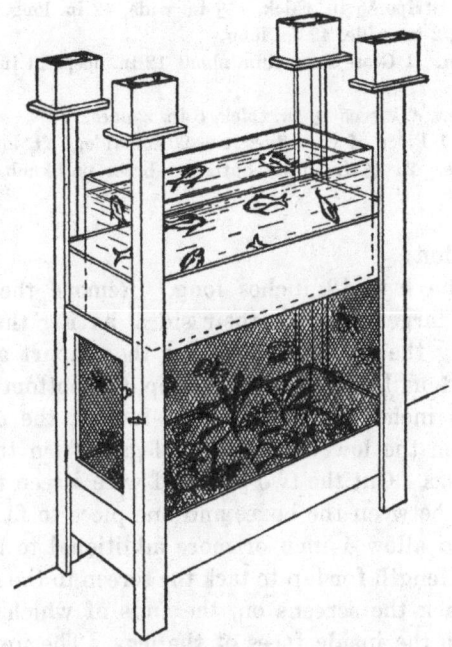

NATURE-STUDY STAND
Illustration 58   *Figure 1*

The space between the upper and lower compartments is inclosed with wire screen. The upper compartment contains an ordinary glass aquarium.

Requirements:
Body. 2 Cereal Boxes (about 6 in. deep, 17½ in. wide, 23 in. long). 4 Salt Boxes (about 4 in. deep, 4 in. square).

Door. 2 Strips ½ in. thick, 2 in. wide, 14½ in. long. 2 Strips ½ in. thick, 2 in. wide, 20 in. long.

Legs. 4 Strips ½ in. thick, 1½ in. wide, 42 in. long. 4 Strips ½ in. thick, 2 in. wide, 42 in. long.

Aquarium. 1 Glass Aquarium about 12 in. deep, 14 in. wide, 20 in. long.

Leg Caps. 4 Pieces ½ in. thick, 5 in. square.

Screen. 1 Piece of wire fly-screen 20 in. wide, 5 ft. long.

Hardware. 2 1 ½ in. brass butts. 1 brass pull-knob. 1 brass button.

Construction:

Make the legs 42 inches long. Remove the covers. Place the large boxes on their sides, having their open tops facing the same way. Space them apart about 18 inches and nail the legs on. Keep the bottom face of one box 4 inches and the bottom face of the other 28 inches from the lower end of the legs. Turn the stand upon its legs. Cut the two pieces of wire screen to fit the side space between the boxes and one piece to fit the end spaces, and allow 1 inch or more additional to both the width and length for lap to tack the screen to the legs and boxes. Tack the screens on, the ends of which may be fastened to the inside faces of the legs. The upper and lower edges may be turned at a right angle and fastened to the boxes. Fasten each corner of the screen first, drawing it smooth and without buckles, then fasten along the edge between. Place the stand on its legs and nail a cap on the projecting top of each leg, setting them square with the legs, and allow them to project 1½ inches on all sides. Make the door 2 inches longer than the height of the space between the boxes, and fit it between the end legs, keeping its outside face even with the outside face of the legs. Fasten the screen on the inside face of and hang the door. Screw on the pull-knob and the button. Set a flower-box on the center of and square with each cap, and fasten it to the cap with small brads driven from inside the box into the cap. Casters may be added if desired.

CHAPTER IX

THREE OR MORE BOXES USED IN SIMPLE COMBINATION

The Bedroom

SOILED-LINEN RECEIVER
DOUBLE WARDROBE   PLANT-STAND
WASHSTAND
MIRROR FRAME   DRESSING-TABLE

Color Scheme:
    Flemish oak (seal brown).
    Old blue.

Woodwork:
    Brown Flemish oak (stained).

Furniture:
    Brown Flemish.

Walls:
    Old blue (light), with motif stenciled in same color as furniture.

Ceiling:
    White.

Hangings:
    Canvas in old blue, with motif stenciled in same color as on the walls.

Curtains:
    White muslin.

Floor:
    Painted same color as furniture; rugs old blue and brown predominating.

Plants:
    Growing plants or cut flowers with white blossoms.

CHAPTER IX

Illustration 59
PHOTOGRAPHIC-MATERIAL STAND
Three boxes placed on end. Covers from all and one end from two removed. One box sawed in halves. Door, shelves, legs, and false top added.

Illustration 60
REFERENCE STAND
One box placed on its side, cover removed. Shelves, legs, and false top added. Two boxes placed on end, covers and one end removed.

Illustration 61
CHILD'S CLOTHES-PRESS
One box placed on its side, cover removed. Two boxes placed on end, cover and one end removed. Shelves, legs, and false top added.

Illustration 62
UMBRELLA- AND OVERSHOE-STAND
One box placed on end. Two boxes placed top side up. Covers from all removed. Shelves, corner trim, and facing strips added.

Illustration 63
CHAFING-DISH TABLE
One box placed top side up, cover removed. Two boxes placed on end. Each has one side removed and hinged as door. Shelves, legs, and false top added.

Illustration 64
WASHSTAND
One box placed top side up, one side removed and hinged as a flap-door. Two boxes placed on end. Each has one side removed and hinged as door. Shelves, legs, and false top added.

Illustration 65
OCTAGON NURSERY TABLE
Four boxes placed on end. Each has one side removed. Shelves, legs, and false top added.

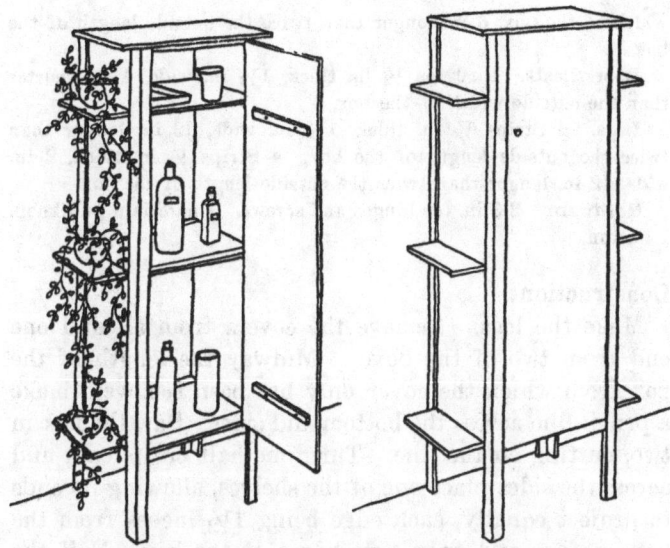

PHOTOGRAPHIC-MATERIAL STAND

Illustration 59   *Figures 1 and 2*

The projecting shelves may be used to hold the printing-frames while making prints. The stand may also be used in the invalid-room for medicines or bandages. When so used, growing plants or small articles may be placed on the projecting shelves.

Requirements:

Body. 3 Butter Boxes (about 10¼ in. deep, 13¾ in. wide, 14¼ in. long).

Shelves. 3 Pieces the same thickness as the sides of the boxes, 12 in. longer than the outside width of the boxes.

Top. 1 Piece 3 in. longer than the end of the box each way.

Door. 1 Piece ½ in. thick, 3 in. less in width than the outside width of the box, 6 in. longer than twice the outside length of the box.

Door Cleats. 2 Strips ½ in. thick, 1½ in. wide, 4 in. shorter than the outside width of the box.

Legs. 4 Strips ½ in. thick, 1½ in. wide, 12 in. longer than twice the outside length of the box. 4 Strips ½ in. thick, 2 in. wide, 12 in. longer than twice the outside length of the box.

Hardware. 2 3 in. tee hinges and screws. 1 porcelain pull-knob. 1 button.

Construction:

Make the legs. Remove the covers from all and one end from two of the boxes. Midway the length of the box from which the cover only has been removed, make a pencil line across the bottom and sides. Saw the box in two, cutting on the line. Turn one half on its end, and across the sides place one of the shelves, allowing its ends to project equally, each edge being 1½ inches from the bottom face and open side edges of the box. Nail the shelf on and cut from the covers two strips 1½ inches wide, and length equal to the inside width of the boxes, and nail them one on each side of the shelf. Cover the open ends of the other two boxes in the same manner. Turn one of the large boxes on the shelf end and place the other large box on its shelf end upon it, with the open compartments facing the same way. Match their edges and nail them together. Do the same with the small box. Nail the top on, allowing it to project equally all around. Turn all the boxes open side down upon the floor and nail on the rear legs. Reverse and nail on the front legs. Nail the cleats on the door, placing them about 4 inches from each end. Fit and hang the door, placing the hinges about 6 inches from each end. Screw on the pull-knob and the button.

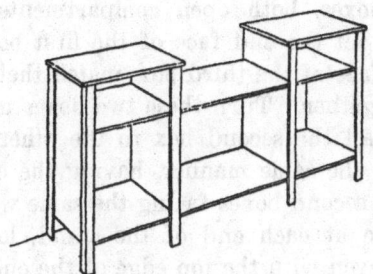

REFERENCE STAND

Illustration 60 *Figure 1*

Requirements:

Body. 3 Soap Boxes (about 10¾ in. deep, 14¼ in. wide, 20 in. long).

Legs. 4 Strips ⅜ in. thick, 1⅜ in. wide, 6 in. longer than the outside length of the boxes. 4 Strips ⅜ in. thick, 1¾ in. wide, 6 in. longer than the outside length of the boxes.

Tops. 2 Pieces ½ in. thick, 2 in. wider than the outside depth of the box with the cover removed, 2 in. longer than the outside width of the box.

Facing Strip Legs. 4 Strips ⅜ in. thick, 1¾ in. wide, 6 in. longer than the outside length of the long boxes.

Construction:

Make the legs 6 inches longer than the length of the boxes. Remove the covers from all and one end from each of two boxes. Use the removed end of each of these boxes as a shelf for each. Stand these two boxes on their closed ends and place and nail the shelves in them at a height to correspond with the top side of the third box when the third box is placed on its side. Stand the third box on end, and upon its upper end place one of the other two boxes, both open compartments facing the same way. Set the end face of the first box even with the outside face of the third box, match their edges, and nail them together. Turn these two boxes upside down; place and nail the second box to the other end of the third box in the same manner, having the open ends of the first and second boxes facing the same way. Nail on the legs, two at each end of the stand, keeping their upper ends even with the top edge of the end sections of the stand. Turn the stand upon its legs and nail a top on each end section, allowing the top to project 5/8 inch over the outside face of the legs at the front, rear, and end. Nail on the facing strip legs, two on the front and two at opposite points on the rear side, so placed that their edges will project evenly over the abutting edges of the boxes.

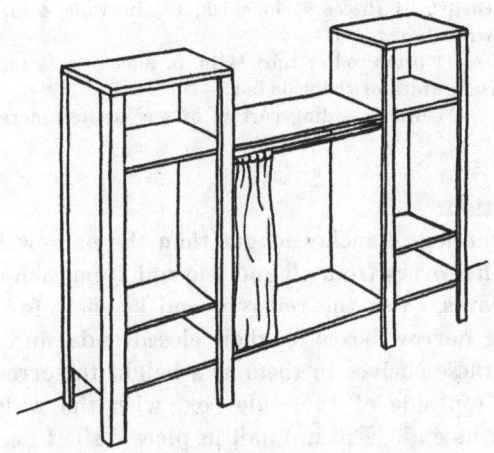

CHILD'S CLOTHES-PRESS

Illustration 61   *Figure 1*

This is similar in form and construction to the Reference Stand, but is made with larger boxes, additional shelves, and a curtain.

Requirements:

Body. 1 Packing Box (about 9¼ in. deep, 28 in. wide, 31 in. long). 2 Tobacco Boxes (about 9¼ in. deep, 13¾ in. wide, 37 in. long).

Tops. 2 Pieces ½ in. thick, 3 in. larger each way than the end of the narrow boxes.

Shelves. 4 Pieces ½ in. thick, width equal to the inside depth of the narrow box, and length equal to the inside length of the narrow box.

Legs. 4 Pieces ⅜ in. thick, 1⅜ in. wide, 4 in. longer than the narrow boxes. 4 Pieces ⅜ in. thick, 1¾ in. wide, 4 in. longer than the narrow boxes.

Facing Strips. 4 Pieces ⅜ in. thick, 1¾ in. wide, 4 in. longer than the narrow boxes.

Hardware. 1 brass rod or tube ¼ in. in diameter, ½ in. longer than the inside width of the wide box.

Curtain. A suitable sliding curtain of any desired material or pattern.

Construction:

Make the legs 4 inches longer than the narrow boxes. Remove the covers from all and one end from each of the narrow boxes. Use the removed end as shelf for each. Stand the narrow boxes on their closed ends, and place and nail these shelves in them at a height to correspond with the top side of the wide box, with the wide box placed on its end. Fit and nail in place a shelf near the other end of each of the narrow boxes, having the compartments at each end of the box the same in size. Lay the wide box on its side and place one of the narrow boxes upon it, both open compartments facing the same way. Set the end face of the narrow box even with the outside end face of the wide box. Match their edges and nail them together. Turn them upside down and nail the other narrow box to the other end of the wide box in the same manner, having the open ends of the narrow boxes facing the same way. Nail on the corner legs, two at each end of the stand, having their upper ends even with the open ends of the boxes. Turn the stand upon its legs, and place and nail a top on each end section, allowing the top to project ⅝ inch over the outside face of the legs at the front, rear, and end. Nail on the facing strips, two on the front and two at opposite points on the rear side, so placed that their edges will project evenly over the abutting edges of the boxes.

Bore a hole ¼ inch in diameter and ¼ inch deep in the inside side face of the wide compartment, 1 inch from the front face and 1 inch from the under side of the top of the compartment. Gouge a vertical slot ¼ inch wide from one hole to the under side of the top of the compartment. Slip the curtain upon the rod and insert one end of the rod in the first hole and spring the other end through the slot into the second hole.

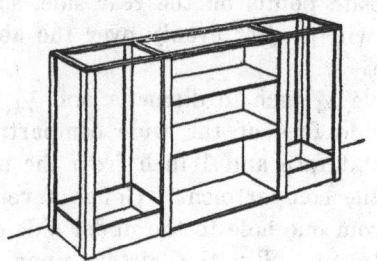

UMBRELLA- AND OVERSHOE-STAND
Illustration 62 *Figure 1*

Requirements:

Body. 1 Grocery Packing Box (about 7¾ in. deep, 21½ in. wide, 31½ in. long). 2 Shoe-polish Boxes (about 5⅝ in. deep, 7½ in. wide, 9⅞ in. long).

Shelves. 2 Pieces ½ in. thick, width equal to the inside depth of the box, length equal to the inside width of the box.

Corner Trim. 4 Strips ½ in. thick, 1¼ in. wide, length equal to the outside length of the large box. 4 Strips ½ in. thick, 1¾ in. wide, length equal to the outside length of the large box.

Vertical Facing Strips. 4 Strips ½ in. thick, 2 in. wide, length equal to the outside length of the large box.

Top Facing Strips. 2 Strips ½ in. thick, 2 in. wide, 1 in. longer than twice the outside length of the small box and the outside width of the large box combined. 4 Strips ½ in. thick, 2 in. wide, 1 in. longer than the outside width of the large box.

Construction:

Make the legs as long as the outside length of the large box. Remove the covers. Fit and nail the shelves in place, making one compartment about 6 inches high, the other two being of equal height. The shelves may be fastened with 1¼ inch brads driven through the side and bottom of the box into the edges of the shelves. Turn the large box on its end on the floor, the large compartment being at the lower end. Place one of the small boxes on the floor against the side of the large box and nail them together. Do the same with the other small box at the other side of the large box. Nail the corner trim on the outer end of each small box, also two vertical facing strips on both the front and the rear on the side edge of the large box. Keep the inner edges of these strips even with the inside face of the side of the large box and their upper ends even with the outside face of the top end. Lay the long top facing strips, flat side down, across the front and rear edge of the stand and nail them. Keep their ends even with the outside face of the corner trim. Their outside edges are also to be even with the outside face of the corner trim and vertical facing strips. Two inches back from each end of these top facing strips make a saw-cut $\frac{1}{4}$ inch deep and, with a chisel, cut away the top half of the strip at this point. Do the same with each end of all the short facing strips. Make two similar saw-cuts 2 inches apart across the top of the long strips, in line with both edges of the four vertical facing strips and cut away in like manner. Place all the short strips in place, the uncut side up, and fit their ends into the recesses cut in the long strips and nail them. These recesses are made and fit like those described for the Picture Frame, Illustration 72.

BOX FURNITURE

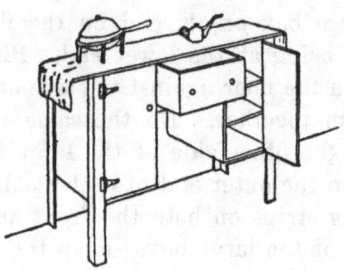

CHAFING-DISH TABLE

Illustration 63   *Figures 1 and 2*

There are two closets on the side and a drawer between. The recess between the side closets is closed at the rear by a junction piece extending 2 inches below the drawer. Each closet contains two shelves.

Requirements:

Body. 2 Canned-tomato Boxes (about 10½ in. deep, 13½ in. wide, 18½ in. long). 1 Canned-asparagus Box (about 8¼ in. deep, 12 in. wide, 14½ in. long).

Doors. 2 Pieces ½ in. thick, width 1½ in. less than the closet box, and length equal to the outside length of the closet box.

Top. 1 Piece ½ in. thick, 2 in. wider than the outside width of the closet boxes, 3 in. longer than the outside length of the drawer box and twice the outside depth of the closet boxes combined.

Shelves. 4 Pieces ½ in. thick, width equal to the outside depth of the closet box, length equal to the inside width of the closet box.

Drawer Guides. 2 Strips ½ in. thick, 2 in. wide, length equal to side width of the closet boxes.

Facing Strips. 1 Strip ½ in. thick, 2 in. wide, length equal to the outside length of the drawer box.

Back Strips. 1 Piece ½ in. thick, 3 in. wider than the outside depth of the drawer box, 3 in. shorter than the outside length of the drawer box and twice the outside depth of the closet boxes combined.

Legs. 4 Strips ½ in. thick, 1½ in. wide, 28 in. long. 4 Strips ½ in. thick, 2 in. wide, 28 in. long.

Hardware. 4 3 in. tee hinges and screws. 4 pull-knobs. 2 small brass hooks and screws. 2 brass screw-eyes.

Construction:

Make the legs 28 inches long. Remove one side from the boxes which are to form the side closets and nail the cover down closely, then fit and fasten in the shelves with brads driven from the outside of the box through into the edges of the shelves, two shelves to each box. Place the drawer box upon the floor, top side up, and remove the cover. Against each end of this box place one of the closets on end, with the open fronts facing the same way. Place the top across the tops of the closets, allowing its rear edge to project ½ inch over the back face of the closets and 1½ inches over each end and the front of the closets, and nail it to them. Turn all three boxes face down on the floor, and move the drawer up against the under side of the top, and nail the rear legs on the outside corners of the closets. Temporarily to hold the rear legs the proper distance apart, place a light strip of wood across the backs of them near their lower ends and fasten slightly to one leg, then draw the legs together until they measure the same distance apart at the bottom as at the top, and nail the strip to the other leg. Nail on the back strip, placing its upper edge against the under side of the top. This back strip will extend across the rear upper ends of both closets between the rear legs, its outside face being even with the outside rear face of the legs. Remove the temporary strips and turn the table upon its back, front side up. Fit the drawer into place and fasten the drawer guides to the side of each closet for the drawer to slide upon, and place a block at the back to prevent its going in too far. Their ends should be even with the front face of the closets before the door is hung. Put the front legs on and hang the doors. Put the temporary strip across the lower ends of the front legs the same as for the back legs, then, with both doors closed, fit the facing strip across the ends of the drawer guides and between the closets under the drawer. The outer face of the facing strip will be even with the outer faces of the drawer and the doors. Screw on the knobs and place a small hook and eye just below the facing strip to keep the doors closed. Remove the temporary strips and stand the table upon its legs.

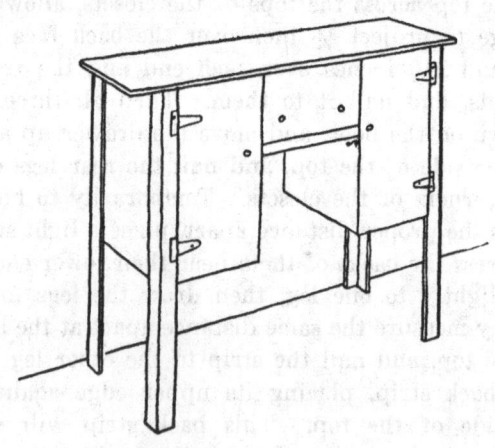

BOX FURNITURE 171

WASHSTAND

Illustration 64   *Figures 1 and 2*

Requirements:

Body. 1 Butter Box (about 10½ in. deep, 13 in. wide, 25 in. long). 2 Condensed-milk Boxes (about 7¼ in. deep, 13 in. wide, 19¾ in. long).

Top. 1 Piece ⅝ in. thick, 7 in. longer and 2 in. wider than the bottom of the box.

Doors. Made from the covers of the boxes.

Small Shelves. 4 Pieces ½ in. thick, width equal to the inside width of the box, and length equal to the inside depth of the box.

Large Shelf. 1 Piece ½ in. thick, about 13 in. wide, 10½ in. long.

Legs. 4 Strips ½ in. thick, 1¼ in. wide, 31 in. long. 4 Strips ½ in. thick, 1¾ in. wide, 31 in. long.

Towel Rods. 2 Child's broom handles.

Curtain Rod. 1 Child's broom handle.

Waterproof Cover. 1 Piece white enameled oil-cloth, 3 in. wider and longer than the top.

Curtain. 1 Piece cloth, ¾ yd. long.

Hardware. 1 package carpet tacks to fasten oil-cloth. 6 brass hinges. 4 brass curtain hooks for towel-rod hangers. 2 brass curtain hooks for curtain-rod hangers. 2 small brass hooks and screw-eyes for fastening the side doors.

Construction:

Make the legs. Place the largest box with its side upon the floor. Put the small boxes upright upon it, one at each end, with the faces even at the end, and nail them to the lower box, driving the nails down through the ends of the small boxes. Clinch them on the under side of the top of the bottom box. Keep all the open compartments of the boxes to the front, and all the faces even with each other.

Make the top of the washstand of two or more boards 7 inches longer and 2 inches wider than the bottom box. Cut a circular hole in the center of the top, suitable for the bowl which rests in it, allowing the edge of the bowl to project about an inch above the top. Sandpaper and smooth the edges of the hole. Then nail the top across the tops of the upper boxes, so that the front edge will project $1\frac{1}{2}$ inches, the ends $3\frac{1}{2}$ inches each, and the rear edge $\frac{1}{2}$ inch beyond the boxes. Make the shelves and fit them in place, securing them with nails driven through the sides of the boxes. The shelf for the waste-water pail should be placed so that the top of the pail will be 3 inches from the top of the washstand.

Nail the legs on the outside corners of the upright boxes, driving the nails into the edges of the upper boxes. Make the doors and hang them. Put the pull-knobs 2 inches from the edges, in the middle of the doors. When finished, the outer faces of the doors and the legs will be even with each other.

Put on the brass hooks and screw in the eyes for fastening the upper doors.

The curtain pole is made of a child's broom handle cut to the proper length and held up by two brass hooks screwed into the under side of the top. The towel racks at each end of the washstand are made of broom handles held by brass hooks placed 3½ inches below the top of the stand.

Cover the top with the white enameled oil-cloth, stretched taut, turned under the edges, and tacked underneath. For the bowl opening, cut a hole much smaller than the opening and slit the edges, turning them back and tacking them on the under side.

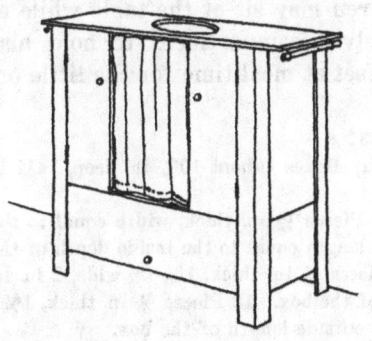

BOX FURNITURE

OCTAGON NURSERY TABLE
Illustration 65   *Figures 1 and 2*

Four children may sit at the table while at play, each having a shelved compartment to hold his toys. The table may be set at meal-time for the little ones.

Requirements:
Body. 4 Soap Boxes (about 10¾ in. deep, 14¼ in. wide, 20 in. long).

Shelves. 12 Pieces ½ in. thick, width equal to the inside width of the box, and length equal to the inside depth of the box.

Legs. 12 Pieces ⅜ in. thick, 1⅜ in. wide, 2 in. longer than the outside length of the box. 12 Pieces ⅜ in. thick, 1¾ in. wide, 2 in. longer than the outside length of the box.

Top. 1 Piece ¾ in. thick, octagon shape 42 in. across from side to side (six boards wide. See Fig. 2).

Construction:
Make the legs 2 inches longer than the outside length of the box. Remove the covers. Fit and nail three shelves in each box, placing the first one 6 inches from one end of the box, the next one 11 inches from the same

end, and divide the balance of the space equally with the third shelf. Fasten the shelves with 1¼ inch wire brads driven from the outside through into the ends of the shelves. Nail two legs on each box at the corners of the open side, allowing them to project 2 inches over the end having the largest compartment. Stand each box on its legs so placed as to form a hollow square in the center, having the open sides face out. (See outline of the boxes in dotted lines in Fig. 2 of the illustration.) Place a small block 2 inches high under the rear end of each

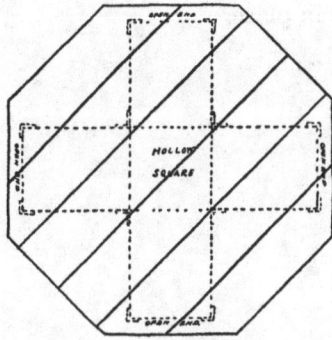

box to make it stand level. Move the boxes together until the corners touch and match. Place the inner legs in a reverse position to fit in each angle, and nail to both boxes forming the angle, using the try-square. Make the top of octagon shape, 42 inches across from side to side. Use seasoned, grooved and tongued material ¾ inch thick, 7 inches wide, planed on both sides. Draw the octagon full size on the floor. Divide the space across in six equal spaces and draw the lines representing the boards as shown in Fig. 2. Lay the boards between the lines and mark and cut them to the proper angle. Place them across the tops of the boxes and nail firmly, driving each tightly against the other, allowing each side edge to project about 1 inch over the outside face of the legs. Set the nail-heads slightly below the top surface, and then finish the top face with the smoothing-plane.

If preferable, the boards forming the top may be joined with hot glue instead of the groove-and-tongue joint, but the edges must be held tightly together about thirty-six hours, or until the glue becomes hard, before nailing the top in place.

CHAPTER X

THE BOX TAKEN PARTLY OR ENTIRELY APART AND
THE MATERIAL USED IN CONSTRUCTION

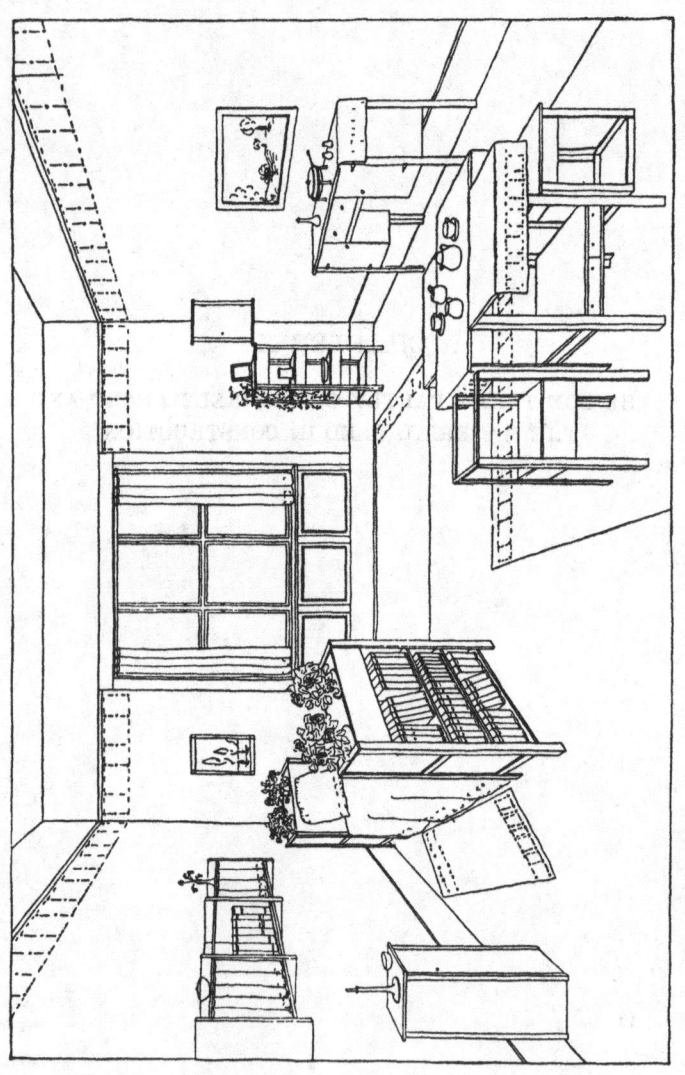

The Studio

"NOTIONETTE" LARGE WALL RACK
WINDOW-SEAT
"SILVERETTE" "DRESSERETTE"
CHAFING-DISH TABLE
GREEK-CROSS TEA-TABLE   DESK CHAIR
CLUB-ROOM STOOL

Color Scheme:
 Black.
 Orange.

Woodwork:
 Black paint.

Furniture:
 Black paint.

Walls:
 Orange, with motif stenciled in orange brighter than the walls, with a touch of black.

Drop Ceiling:
 Same color as walls, but much lighter shade.

Hangings, Table- and Couch-covers:
 Dark green, with motif stenciled in black and orange.

Curtains:
 Net in light orange or green, with small motif stenciled in black.

Floor:
 Painted black, with rugs in Oriental colors.

Plants:
 Vines and growing plants with orange-colored or deep red blossoms.

CHAPTER X

Illustration 66
KETTLE- AND COVER-HOLDER
One box placed on side. Cover and one end removed.

Illustration 67
NEST OF BENCHES
Seven boxes placed top side up. Both sides and the cover removed from each, and one thicker side and corner cleats added.

Illustration 68
TABLE BOOKSTAND
One box placed top side up. Cover and one side removed. Legs and handle arms added.

Illustration 69
FIREWOOD OR NEWSPAPER RACK
One box placed top side up. Cover and both sides removed. Side braces, legs, and handle arms added.

Illustration 70
DRESSING-TABLE CHAIR
One box placed top side up. Cover, one side, and partitions of both ends removed. Legs and finish trims added.

Illustration 71
FLAG WALL RACK
Four boxes placed on their sides. Covers and both sides of each box removed. Three sides used as shelves. Bottom partitions and facing strips added.

Illustration 72
PICTURE FRAME NO. 1
One side removed from a packing box of ¾ inch wood.

Illustration 73

MIRROR FRAME

The same as Illustration 72.

Illustration 74

PICTURE FRAME NO. 2

Both sides removed from a 40-inch packing box.

Illustration 75

"DRESSERETTE"

One box taken apart and the materials used in construction.

Illustration 76

GREEK-CROSS TEA-TABLE

Two boxes placed top side up with covers removed. Portions of three other boxes used.

Illustration 77

CHILD'S BEDSTEAD

One box placed top side up, cover removed. Legs and framework added.

Illustration 78

INVALID'S BED-TABLE

One box placed top side up. One end removed and hinged as door. Shelves, revolving portion, legs, and top added.

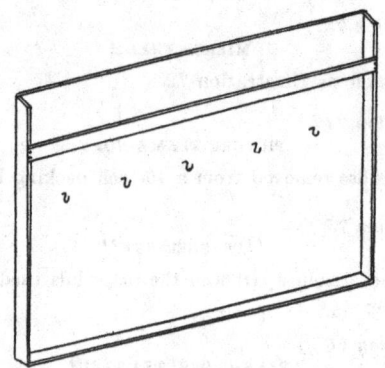

KETTLE- AND COVER-HOLDER

Illustration 66 *Figure 1*

Requirements:

Body. 1 Window-glass Box (about 2½ in. deep, 21 in. wide, 31 in. long).

End Strips. 2 Strips ½ in. thick, 1 in. wide, and length equal to the outside width of the box.

Bottom Strip. 1 Strip ½ in. thick, 1 in. wide, and length 1 in. shorter than the outside length of the box.

Brace. 1 Strip ½ in. thick, 1½ in. wide, and length equal to the outside length of the box.

Hardware. 6 brass hooks. The end strips, bottom strip, and brace may be made from the side.

Construction:

Remove the cover and one side. Nail one end strip placed on its edge across each end (and both on the same side) of the cover. Keep the outside face and the ends of the strip even with the edges of the cover. Nail the bottom strip, also placed on its edge, extending from one end strip to the other and along the lower edge of the holder. Place the brace across the end strip. Screw the hooks into the body of the holder just below the brace at points best suited for the various sizes of frying and sauce pans. The covers placed behind the brace are supported by their knob handles resting upon the top edge of the brace.

184   BOX FURNITURE

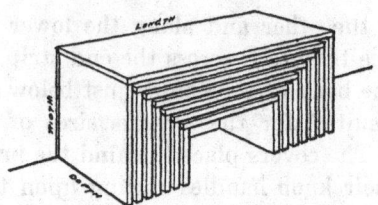

NEST OF BENCHES FOR KINDERGARTEN AND SETTLEMENT

Illustration 67   *Figure 1*

This simple device is an excellent substitute for extra chairs. The set has a seating capacity for nine persons, seating them according to age or size, two children being seated upon each of the two larger benches. Two sets were used constantly in the Sunshine Cottages.

The outside dimensions of the finished seats are as follows:

1 seat	8	in. deep,	9	in. wide,	16	in. long
1 "	8½	"	10	"	18	"
1 "	9	"	11	"	20	"
1 "	9½	"	12	"	22	"
1 "	10	"	13	"	24	"
1 "	10½	"	14	"	26	"
1 "	11	"	15	"	28	"

The benches are made from boxes by removing the covers and sides, one side being replaced with a thicker piece forming the seat.

Requirements:

Bodies. 7 Boxes varying in size, but each sufficiently large to make one of the benches. The ends of the boxes must be ¾ in. thick and the bottoms not more than ½ in. thick.

BOX FURNITURE

Seats.
1 piece	¾ in. thick,	8	in. wide,	16 in. long.
1 "	¾ "	8½	"	18	"
1 "	¾ "	9	"	20	"
1 "	¾ "	9½	"	22	"
1 "	¾ "	10	"	24	"
1 "	¾ "	10½	"	26	"
1 "	¾ "	11	"	28	"

Construction:

Remove the covers and both sides from the boxes, and reduce the remaining portion of each box to form a bench. The following table specifies the outside dimensions of each body-piece before the addition of the seat.

1 body-piece	8 in. deep,	8¼ in. wide,	16 in. long
1 "	8½ "	9¼ "	18 "
1 "	9 "	10¼ "	20 "
1 "	9½ "	11¼ "	22 "
1 "	10 "	12¼ "	24 "
1 "	10½ "	13¼ "	26 "
1 "	11 "	14¼ "	28 "

Nail a seat to each body-piece of a corresponding size, using care to have the ends of the body-piece square with the bottom, which then becomes the back of the bench. Use 2 inch wire nails to secure the seat to the ends. When completed, the benches should all fit one within the other as shown. Paint or stain them any color, dark green being suggested as serviceable.

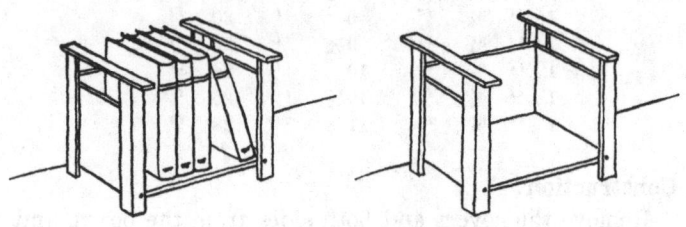

TABLE BOOKSTAND

Illustration 68 *Figures 1 and 2*

Requirements:

Body. 1 Bluing Box, 6⅝ in. deep, 11⅛ in. wide, 13 in. long.

Legs. 4 Strips ⅜ in. thick, 1⅛ in. wide, 4 in. longer than the height of the box. 4 Strips ⅜ in. thick, 1½ in. wide, 4 in. longer than the height of the box.

Handle Arms. 2 Strips ⅝ in. thick, 1½ in. wide, 3 in. longer than the width of the box.

Construction:

Make the legs 4 inches longer than the height of the box. Remove the cover and one side of the box. Place a leg at each corner and nail firmly, allowing each leg to project 2 inches both above and below the box. Set the heads of the nails well in and clinch the points on the inside. Use a light hammer and the brad-awl if necessary, as the material, being thin, is liable to split. Place the handle arms flat side down on top of and across the legs, having the outer edge even with the outside face of the legs, each end projecting equally over the front and rear face of the legs. Use long, slender wire brads for securing the handle arms to the legs, driven from the top through the arms into the tops of the legs. Do not fail to place a well-driven nail through the front legs into the edge of the bottom, as indicated by the dots in the illustration.

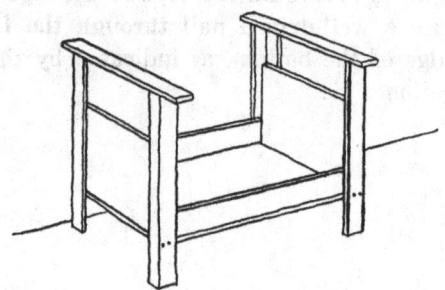

FIREWOOD OR NEWSPAPER RACK
Illustration 69   *Figure 1*

Requirements:

Body. 1 Condensed-milk Box (about 7¼ in. deep, 13 in. wide, 19¾ in. long).

Legs. 4 Strips ½ in. thick, 1½ in. wide, 8 in. longer than the height of the box. 4 Strips ½ in. thick, 2 in. wide, 8 in. longer than the height of the box.

Handle Arms. 2 Strips ¾ in. thick, 2 in. wide, 5 in. longer than the width of the box.

Side Braces. 2 Strips ½ in. thick, 2½ in. wide, and the length equal to the length of the box inside.

Construction:

Make the legs 8 inches longer than the height of the box with the cover removed. Remove the cover and both sides of the box. Turn the remaining portion on its side and nail the legs of one side in position. Turn the box over and secure the legs of the other side, allowing each leg to project 4 inches above and 4 inches below the box. Place the try-square on the bottom and against the end to square it, then drive a nail through the legs into the edge of the bottom at the points shown by the dots, to hold it square. Having made both ends square and secure, place the rack upright on its legs, and cut the side braces to the neat inside length between the ends. Place them on edge inside and secure with nails driven through the legs from the outside, and clinch the nails on the inside face of the brace. Place the handle arms on top of the legs, having their outer edges even with the outside face of the legs, and project the ends equally outside of the legs both front and rear. Use long, slender wire nails for securing the handle arms to the legs, driven from the top through the arms into the legs.

BOX FURNITURE

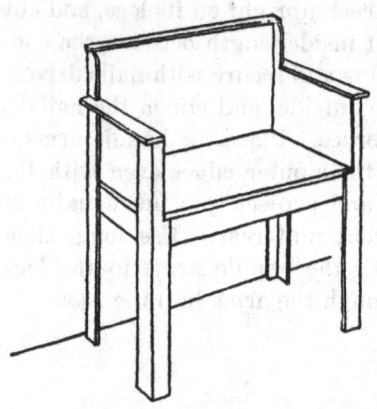

DRESSING-TABLE CHAIR
Illustration 70   *Figure 1*

The children's chairs shown in the Nursery Interior and the baby's high chair in the Dining-room Interior are a smaller type of this chair made with smaller boxes, the former having shorter and the latter longer legs.

Requirements:
Body. 1 Canned-soup Box (about 11 in. deep, 13½ in. wide, 18¼ in. long).

Legs. 2 Strips ½ in. thick, 1½ in. wide, 21 in. long. 2 Strips ½ in. thick, 2 in. wide, 21 in. long. 2 Strips ½ in. thick, 1½ in. wide, 25 in. long. 2 Strips ½ in. thick, 2 in. wide, 25 in. long.

Back Top. 1 Strip ½ in. thick, 2 in. wide, 19¼ in. long.

Arms. 2 Strips ½ in. thick, 1¾ in. wide, 14 in. long.

Seat Support. 2 Strips ½ in. thick, 3 in. wide, 13½ in. long. 1 Strip ½ in. thick, 3 in. wide, 17¼ in. long.

Construction:

Make the legs, two 21 inches and two 25 inches long. Remove the cover and one side from the box. Cut each end down to a height of 6 inches. Nail on the legs, allowing them all to project 15 inches below the bottom (which is to form the seat) of the box. Place a seat support under each end, having its edge against the bottom, and nail both ends to the legs. Place the other support across between the front legs and nail it firmly. Stand the chair upon its legs. Trim the top edges of the back and the back legs until they are even, and nail on the back top. Saw off that portion of each front leg above the seat which projects inside the end face of the body of the chair, and fit and nail the arms on, having their inside edges even with the inside face of the body. It will be necessary to cut the rear end of the arm to let the rear leg in even with the inside edge of the arm. The front end of the arm may project ½ inch over the face of the leg.

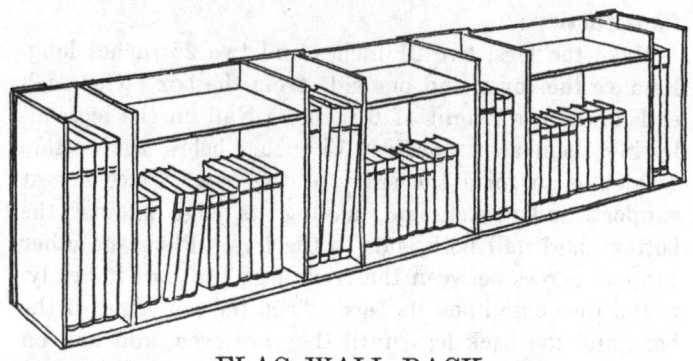

FLAG WALL RACK
Illustration 71   *Figure 1*

The collection of national flags, as seen in the Dining-room Interior, is a pleasing Scandinavian custom. An additional charm is added to the dining-table when, as guest, your country's colors blend in decoration with those of your host. The rack may also be used for pottery or plants, or the open pockets for books, as in the Den Interior.

Requirements:
Body. 3 Condensed-milk Boxes (about 7¼ in. deep, 13 in. wide, 19¾ in. long).

Bottom. 1 Piece ¾ in. thick, width equal to the outside depth of the box, 10¼ in. longer than three times the outside length of the box.

Facing Strips. 2 Pieces ½ in. thick, 3½ in. wide, the length equal to the inside width of the box.

Junction Strips. 2 Pieces ½ in. thick, 7 in. wide, the length equal to the inside width of the box.

End Shelves. 2 Pieces ½ in. thick, the width equal to the inside depth of the box, and 12¾ in. long.

Middle Shelf. 1 Piece ½ in. thick, the width equal to the inside depth of the box, and 18¼ in. long.

Pocket Partitions. 2 Pieces ¾ in. thick, the width equal to the inside depth of the box, and length equal to the inside width of the box. The ends from a fourth condensed-milk box will serve for pocket partitions.

Construction:

Remove the cover and both sides from each box. Stand the remaining portion of all the boxes in a line end to end on their sides, with the end and bottom edges up, having the bottoms all facing the same way, and lay the rack bottom piece across the ends upon them, and nail it to the end edge of the end boxes, having the end of the rack bottom even with the outside end face of the boxes, and allow it to project ½ inch over the outside bottom face of the boxes. Set the third box midway between

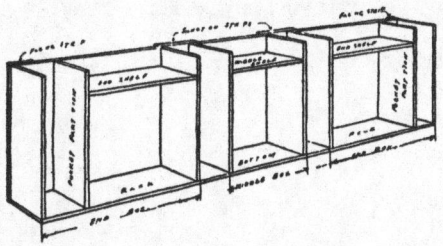

the other two, with the same projection of rack bottom over the bottom face of the box, and nail the rack bottom to the bottom edge of the box. With the try-square set each end of each box square, and at the same time nail through the rack bottom into their ends. Turn the piece over so that the bottoms of all three boxes face up. Nail on the junction pieces which join the bottoms together, and at each end nail the facing strips on the back, having the edge of the facing strips even with the ends of the rack. Turn the rack right side up and fit and nail in place the pocket partitions and shelves, keeping the tops of the shelves 3 inches below the top edge of the rack, and the pockets all of an even width of about 5⅛ inches.

The rack may be hung with picture wire and hooks or nailed to the wall, as circumstances permit.

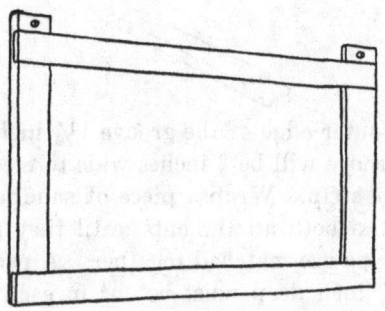

PICTURE FRAME No. 1

Illustration 72 *Figure 1*

Requirements:

Body. 2 Strips ¾ in. thick, 3 in. wide, 23¼ in. long. 2 Strips ¾ in. thick, 3 in. wide, 33 in. long.

Glass. 1 Glass 16 in. by 26 in.

Back. 1 Stiff Pasteboard, 16 in. by 26 in. 1 Piece heavy brown paper, 18 in. by 28 in.

Construction:

The frame is quite easy to make, but care should be taken to make the joints a good close fit. Plane the strips true and smooth, and cut the ends perfectly square. The longer strips should measure exactly 33 inches long; the shorter ones 23¼ inches long. Halve both ends of the longer ones 3 inches back, thus:

and halve one end of each of the shorter ones in the same

manner, and groove out the other end of each of the shorter ones, thus:

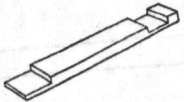

keeping the outer edge of the groove 1¼ inches from the end. The groove will be 3 inches wide to receive the end of the longer strip. Wrap a piece of sandpaper around a block, and smooth all the cuts until they fit perfectly when the strips are matched together. A rabbet ¼ inch wide and ¼ inch deep must be cut in each strip along the edge, forming the opening to receive the glass, picture, and pasteboard backing, thus:

making the short strips right- and left-handed.

Fit all the pieces together and mark and cut the rabbet in the long strips, which will be along the edge on the uncut side of the strip. Lay both long strips flat on their backs, parallel with each other and about 16 inches apart. Coat each joint with hot glue and fit the side strips in place, and hold each corner tightly together with a screw clamp. If no clamps are convenient, put a weight (a flatiron, for instance) upon each corner after first using the try-square to square it. Or the frame may be fastened at the joints with four short screws set in from the back, the length of which must be slightly less than the thickness of the frame. Insert glass, picture, and pasteboard back, and secure with small tacks. Stretch brown paper over the entire back, and glue or paste its edges to the frame.

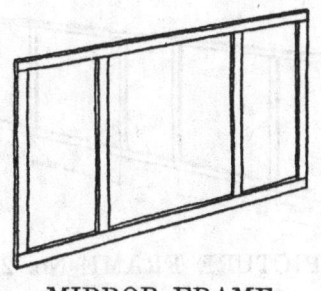

MIRROR FRAME

Illustration 73   *Figure 1*

Requirements:

Body. 2 Strips ¾ in. thick, 3 in. wide, 38½ in. long. 3 Strips ¾ in. thick, 3 in. wide, 19½ in. long.

Mirrors. 1 Mirror Glass, 14 in. square. 2 Mirror Glasses, 7 in. wide, 14 in. long.

Backs. 1 Sheet of stiff pasteboard, 14 in. square. 2 Sheets of stiff pasteboard, 7 in. wide, 14 in. long.

Construction:

Halve the ends of all the strips. Each long strip must have two grooves ⅜ inch deep and 3 inches wide to receive the intermediate strips. The outer edge of these grooves will be 9½ inches from each end of the long strips. Cut a rabbet all around the inside edge of the frame and on both edges of the intermediate strips. For instructions, see description of Picture Frame No. 1, Illustration 72.

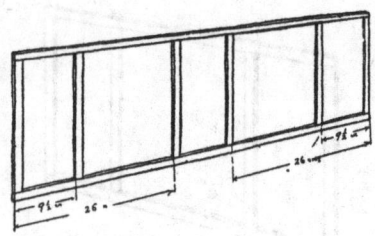

PICTURE FRAME No. 2

Illustration 74   *Figure 1*

Requirements:

Body. 2 Strips ¾ in. thick, 3 in. wide, 64½ in. long. 6 Strips ¾ in. thick, 3 in. wide, 19½ in. long.

Glass. 2 Clear Window-glasses, 14 in. square.

Back. 2 Sheets of stiff pasteboard, 14 in. square. 3 Sheets of stiff pasteboard 7 in. wide, 14 in. long. 2 Pieces heavy brown paper, 15 in. square. 3 Pieces heavy brown paper, 8 in. wide, 15 in. long.

Construction:

Halve the ends of all the strips. Each long strip must have four grooves ⅜ inch deep and 3 inches wide to receive the intermediate strips. The outer edge of the first groove will be 9½ inches from the end of the strip, and the second one will be 26 inches. Cut a rabbet all around the inside edge of the frame and on both edges of the intermediate strips. For instructions, see description of Picture Frame No. 1. Illustration 72.

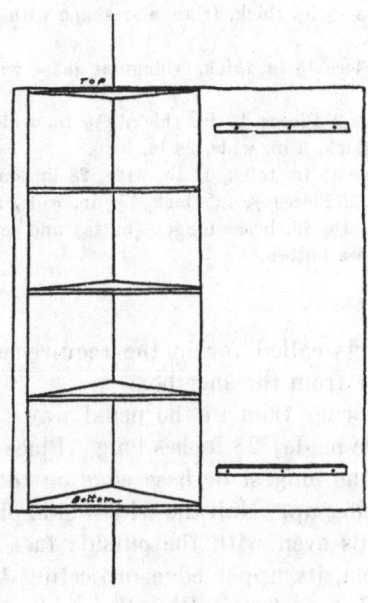

"DRESSERETTE"

Illustration 75   *Figure 1*

This little "Dresserette" was used in a studio for a year in place of a dressing-table, and, as it was secured to the wall in the corner of the room, no floor space was required for it.

Requirements:

Body. 1 Shoe Box (about 14 in. deep, 21 in. wide, 34 in. long).

Sides. 2 Pieces ½ in. thick, one 12¾ in. and one 13¼ in. wide, each 28 in. long.

Shelves. 3 Pieces ½ in. thick, triangular shape with 1 in. added to the depth.

BOX FURNITURE

Top. 1 Piece ½ in. thick, triangular shape with 1 in. added to the depth.

Bottom. 1 Piece ½ in. thick, triangular shape with 1 in. added to the depth.

Corner Trim. 2 Pieces ½ in. thick, 1½ in. wide, 28 in. long. 2 Pieces ½ in. thick, 2 in. wide, 28 in. long.

Door. 1 Piece ½ in. thick, 15 in. wide, 28 in. long.

Door Cleats. 2 Pieces ⅜ in. thick, 1½ in. wide, 14 in. long.

Hardware. 2 1¾ in. brass hinges (butts) and screws. 1 brass pull-knob. 1 brass button.

Construction:

Cut the parts called for in the requirements (except the hardware) from the shoe box.

Make the corner trim in the usual way (the same as corner legs are made) 28 inches long. Place the top and bottom with the longest or base edge on the bench, the triangle pointing up. Nail the widest side piece to them, having its ends even with the outside face of both the top and bottom, its upper edge projecting ½ inch over the points. Fit and nail the other side piece on the opposite edge of the triangles. Turn the piece over, laying it on one of the sides, and fit the shelves in, spacing

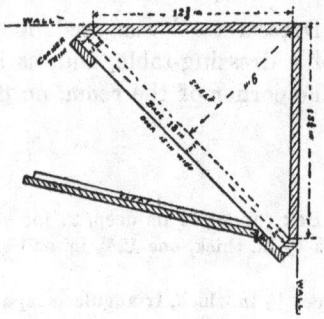

them equally between the ends, using the try-square to make them true.

Plane the edge of the short legs of the corner trim until they fit on each corner, as shown in Fig. 2, and nail them in place. Nail the cleats across the door, putting one 3 inches from each end. Fit and hang the door and screw the pull-knob and button on. Fig. 2 shows the base of the triangle to be 18 inches, the height 9 inches, and the length of each side 12¾ inches. Before cutting, 1 inch is added to the front of the shelf to receive the corner trim.

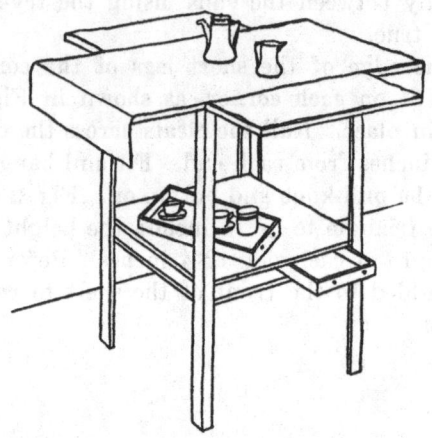

GREEK-CROSS TEA-TABLE

Illustration 76 *Figures 1 and 2*

This unique tea-table is most convenient for a small space. It may be used as a serving-table. The two drawers are used for holding spoons or flat silver or as trays for serving. The lower compartment is open on opposite sides, the other two sides being closed. The drawers extend through, with pull-knobs on both ends. The leaves are hinged and fold. When in use, the leaves are held up by swiveled arms secured to the under side of the table top.

Requirements:
  Body. 1 Packing-box (about 19 in. square, 26 in. long). 2 Raisin Boxes.
  Top. 1 Piece ⅝ in. thick, 18 in. square.
  Drawer Shelves. 2 Pieces ⅜ in. thick, 17¼ in. square.

Leaves. 4 Pieces ⅝ in. thick, 7 in. wide, 18 in. long.

Shelf Separators. 2 Pieces ⅜ in. thick, 1½ in. wide, 17¼ in. long.

Arms. 4 Pieces ¾ in. thick, 1¼ in. wide, 9 in. long.

Legs. 4 Strips ⅜ in. thick, 1⅜ in. wide, 25 in. long. 4 Strips ⅜ in. thick, 1¾ in. wide, 25 in. long.

Hardware. 8 1½ in. brass butts and screws. 4 small brass knobs. 4 screws ¼ in. in diameter and 1⅜ in. long.

Construction:

Select a packing-box whose ends are ⅝ inch thick, and use one end for the table top, and cut the drawer shelf and leg strips from the sides and cover. Make the legs 25 inches long. Make the top 18 inches square, each edge being perfectly straight and smooth. Make the two shelves 17¼ inches square. Lay them upon the bench, with the grain of the wood of both shelves running in the same direction. Place the separators on edge at opposite sides between them and at right angles to and across the grain of the wood of the shelves. Nail both shelves to them with 1½ inch brads driven through the shelf into the edge of the separator, having the outside face and ends of the separator even with the edges of the shelves. Turn them upon edge and nail a leg at each corner, allowing all the legs to project 10 inches on the same side. Stand on its legs and put on the top, nailing it to the top of each leg, having the edges of the top even with the outside face of the legs all around. Place the brass butts about 3 inches each way from each corner, cutting away the edges sufficiently to let the butts in even with the edges of the top. Fit the leaves, letting the butts into their edges in the same way, and hang them. Bore a ¼ inch hole through the center of each arm 4 inches from one end, and counter-bore one side of each so that the head of the screw will go in even. Turn the table upside down and screw the arms on the under side of the top, placing the screw 1 inch from each edge, and midway in the opposite direction. Make the trays from the raisin boxes and fit them between the legs, cutting them down and moving in their sides and ends if necessary. Screw two knobs on each end of each tray, placing them 1¾ inches from each side edge, or about 4 inches apart.

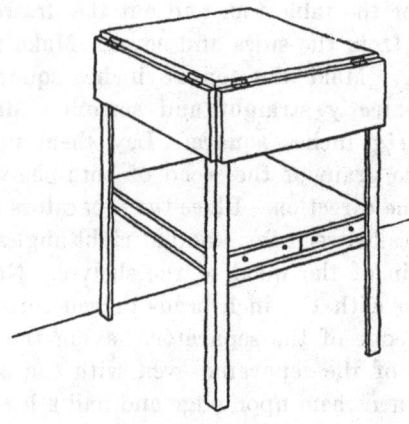

CHILD'S BEDSTEAD

Illustration 77   *Figure 1*

Requirements:

Body. 1 Packing-box (about 15¼ in. deep, 26½ in. wide, 51 in. long).

Legs. 4 Strips ½ in. thick, 1½ in. wide, 36 in. long. 4 Strips ½ in. thick, 2 in. wide, 36 in. long.

Top Frame Side. 2 Strips ½ in. thick, 2 in. wide, 51 in. long. 2 Strips ½ in. thick, 2 in. wide, 54 in. long.

Top Frame End. 2 Strips ½ in. thick, 2 in. wide, 25½ in. long. 2 Strips ½ in. thick, 2 in. wide, 29½ in. long.

Side Slats. 38 Strips ½ in. thick, 1½ in. wide, 22 in. long.

Facing Strips. 2 Strips ½ in. thick, 2 in. wide, 48 in. long. 2 Strips ½ in. thick, 2 in. wide, 23½ in. long.

Construction:

Make the legs 34 inches long. Take the box apart and reduce the depth to 7 inches outside depth without the cover. Put the box together again and turn it on its side. Nail on the legs, allowing them to project 12 inches below the bottom face of the box. and 17 inches above the open top edge. Place it upon its legs and nail on the facing strips along the bottom of the sides and ends, having the bottom edge of the strips even with the bottom face of the box. Nail the 51-inch-long strip to the inside face of the legs, extending it from leg to leg at opposite ends, having its upper edge even with the top of the legs. Put the other one on the opposite side, and put the 25½-inch-long strips across the ends. Miter the ends of the other top frame strips to an angle of 45 degrees and place them on their flat sides on the other top frame strips, having their inner edges even with the inner face of the lower top frame strip, and nail them together. Place the slats on the outside face of the box, with their lower ends resting on the facing strips, having their upper ends on the outside face of the top frame to which they are to be nailed. Place and nail all the slats, spacing them equally 2 inches apart.

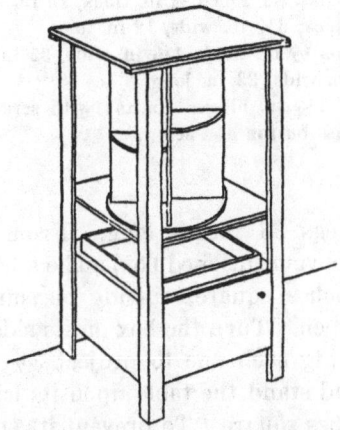

INVALID'S BED-TABLE
Illustration 78 *Figure 1*

The table has a lower compartment, having one door for night conveniences, upon which rests a tea-tray for serving tea or a light luncheon. The upper section contains a revolving rack fitted with shelves carrying the articles most frequently required by the invalid, who turns the rack at will.

Requirements:
Body. 1 Household-ammonia Box (about 10¾ in. deep, 18½ in. wide, 18½ in. long).
Door. Made from the side removed from the box.
Tray. Made from parts of a box 14½ in. square.
Shelf. 1 Piece ½ in. thick, 18½ in. square.
Top. 1 Piece ½ in. thick, 21½ in. square.
Circular Heads. 2 Heads about 13 in. in diameter removed from a half barrel.

Vertical Divisions. 1 Piece ½ in. thick, 13 in. wide, 12 in. long. 2 Pieces ½ in. thick, 6¼ in. wide, 12 in. long.

Legs. 4 Strips ½ in. thick, 1½ in. wide, 33 in. long. 4 Strips ½ in. thick, 2 in. wide, 33 in. long.

Hardware. 2 1½ in. hinges (butts) with screws. 1 porcelain pull-knob. 1 brass button and screw.

Construction:

Make the legs 33 inches long. From the material forming the above-mentioned box, make a box 10¾ inches deep, 18½ inches square, outside measurements, with one side left open. Turn the box on its side and nail the legs on, allowing each one to project 3½ inches below the bottom, and stand the table upon its legs. Make the shelf 18½ inches square. To prevent its splitting, put a cleat ½ inch thick, 1½ inches wide, across each end. Make the revolving shelf rack by standing the wide division-piece on end, and upon it place one of the heads, with the end of the partition extending exactly across the center of the head, and nail them together. On each side of the wide division and at a right angle, place also on end one of the narrow divisions and nail through the head into its end. Turn the piece upside down and place and nail the other head in a similar manner to the other ends of the division-pieces. Fit a shelf (having its outer edge curved the same as the heads) in three of the compartments and place and secure them at varying heights to suit any of the small articles that an invalid would require. Cut off the heads of two 3 inch wire nails, and with the awl make a hole a little smaller than the nail through the center of each head, and drive the headless nail into the hole in each head, allowing each nail to project ¾ inch, which completes the rack. Enter the shelf between the legs at their upper ends, and lower and nail it, the distance between its upper face and the top of the legs being 1/4 inch greater than the outside length of the revolving rack. Bore a hole (slightly larger than the headless nail) through the exact center of the shelf. Put a small leather or metal washer (metal is better) 1/4 inch thick directly over the hole in the shelf, and set the rack in place with the headless nail projecting through the washer into the hole in the shelf. Make the top 21 1/2 inches square; put a cleat 1/2 inch thick, 1 1/2 inches wide, on the under side across each end. Keep each end and the outside edge of the cleat 1 1/2 inches from the outside edge of the top, and it will come between and inside of the projecting legs when the top is nailed on. Bore a hole in the center of the top to receive the headless nail projecting from the top of the rack, and nail on the top, allowing it to project on all sides 1 inch over the outer face of the legs. Fit and hang the door. Screw on the knob and button. Make a tray 14 1/2 inches square of material 3/8 inch thick. It should be about 2 inches deep on the outside.

CHAPTER XI

MORE ELABORATE COMBINATIONS OF THE ARTICLES IN THE PREVIOUS CHAPTERS AND WITH LARGER AND A GREATER NUMBER OF BOXES

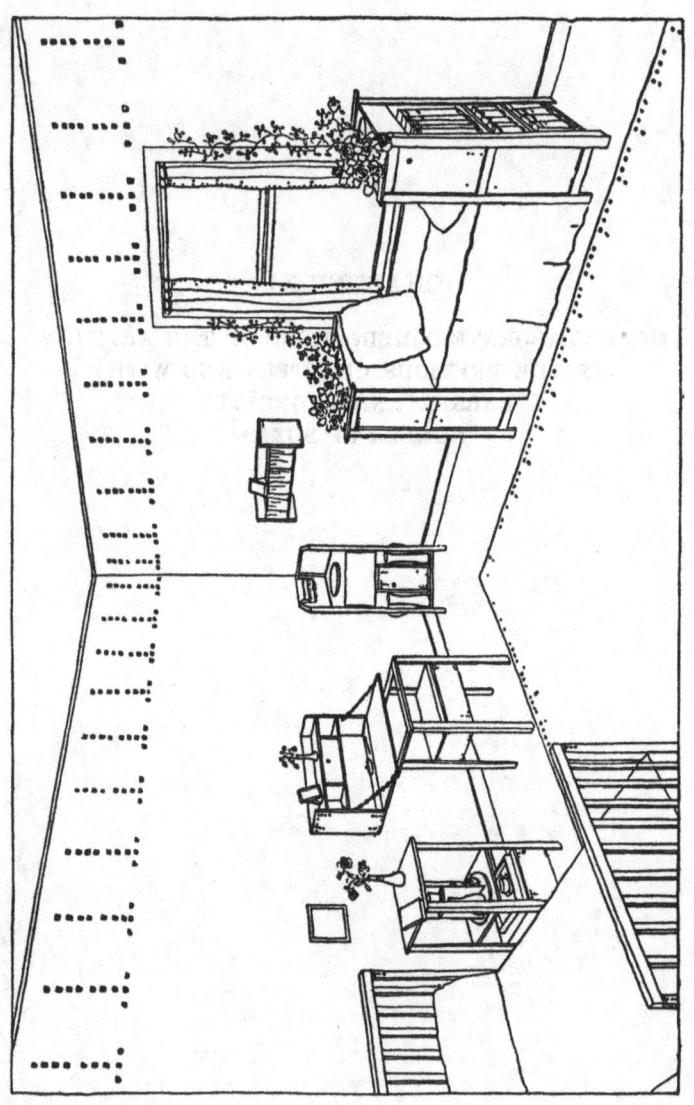

The Invalid's Room

INVALID'S BED TABLE   WALL DESK AND CHAIR
CORNER WASHSTAND   SMALL WALL RACK
WINDOW-SEAT

Color Scheme:
   White.
   Old rose.

Woodwork:
   White paint.

Furniture:
   White paint, with motif stenciled in old rose.

Walls:
   Old rose. with motif stenciled in white.

Ceiling:
   White.

Hangings and Window-seat Cover:
   Linen in old-rose color.

Curtains and Bedspread:
   White dotted swiss. The motif may be expressed by embroidering the dots in groups with old-rose silk.

Floor:
   Light wood, left in its natural state and varnished, with rugs of old rose and white.

Plants:
   Growing ivy, white and rose-colored geraniums, and deep pink roses.

CHAPTER XI

Illustration 79

TEACHER'S DESK

Two large boxes placed on end. Covers removed and hinged as doors. Two small boxes placed on end, covers removed. Corner trim, shelves, brace, and false top added.

Illustration 80

BOY'S WORK-TABLE

Two boxes placed on end. Covers removed and hinged as doors. One box placed top side up, cover removed. Shelves, corner trim, and false top added.

Illustration 81

WINDOW-SEAT

Four boxes placed on their sides. Covers of all and one side of two removed. One box placed on end, the other end removed. Shelves, legs, facing strips, and seat added.

Illustration 82

BEDROOM WINDOW-SEAT

Two boxes placed on end. Covers removed and hinged as doors. One end of each removed. Two boxes placed top side up, covers removed. Lids, shelves, and legs added.

Illustration 83

COLLEGE CORNER SEAT

Four boxes placed on their sides. Covers of all and one side of two removed. Two boxes placed on end, other end removed. One box placed top side up. Shelves, legs, trims, and seat added.

Illustration 84

SINGLE WARDROBE

Two boxes placed top side up. One has side removed and hinged as flap-door, one has end removed. One box placed on end, cover removed. Shelf, door, legs, and false top added.

Illustration 85
DOUBLE WARDROBE
Four boxes placed top side up. Two have one side removed and hinged as flap-door, two have ends removed. Two boxes placed on end, covers removed. Shelf, doors, legs, and false top added.

Illustration 86
SPITZBERGEN SIDEBOARD
Two boxes placed on end and one box on its side. Covers of all removed and hinged as doors. One box placed top side up, cover removed. Partitions, shelves, legs, false top, and plate rack added.

Illustration 87
ALLENDALE SIDEBOARD
Four boxes placed on their sides. Covers and one side of two removed. Covers of two hinged as doors. Shelves, legs, false top, and plate rack added.

Illustration 88
COPENHAGEN SIDEBOARD
Four boxes placed on end. Covers of two removed. Sides of two removed and hinged as doors. Two small boxes placed on end, covers removed and hinged as doors. One box placed on its side, cover removed. Shelves, legs, and false top added.

BOX FURNITURE

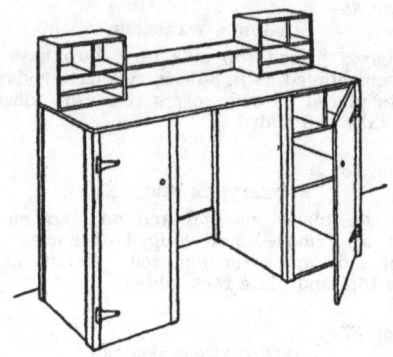

TEACHER'S DESK

Illustration 79   *Figure 1*

Requirements:

Closets. 2 Rubber-shoe Cases (about 13½ in. deep, 14½ in. wide, 27½ in. long).

Pigeonholes. 2 Cocoa Boxes (5 in. deep, 8½ in. wide, 11 in. long).

Closet Shelves. 4 Pieces ½ in. thick, width equal to the inside width of the box, and length equal to the inside depth of the box.

Partitions. 2 Pieces ½ in. thick, 6 in. wide, and length equal to the inside depth of the box.

Corner Trim. 8 Pieces ½ in. thick, 1½ in. wide, and length equal to the outside length of the box. 8 Pieces ½ in. thick, 2 in. wide, and length equal to the outside length of the box.

Top. 1 Piece ⅝ in. thick, 1½ in. wider than the outside depth of the box, and 42 in. long.

Brace. 1 Piece ½ in. thick, 6 in. wide, and 36 in. long.

Pigeonhole Shelves. 4 Pieces ⅜ in. thick, the width equal to the inside depth of the box, and length equal to the inside length of the box. 2 Pieces ⅜ in. thick, 4 in. wide, and length equal to the inside depth of the box.

Long Shelf. 1 Piece ½ in. thick, the width equal to the outside depth of the box with the cover removed, and about 22 in. long.

Door Cleats. 4 Pieces ½ in. thick, 2 in. wide, 5 in. shorter than the outside width of the box.

Doors. The doors will be made from covers removed from the boxes.

Hardware. 2 pull-knobs. 4 3 in. tee hinges and screws.

Construction:

Make the corner trim (same construction as described for legs) the same length as the outside length of the box. Remove the covers. Turn one of the larger boxes open side up, and fit the lower shelf in place (snug fit), placing it in the center of the length of the box, and secure it by driving 1¼ inch brads through the sides of the box directly into the edges of the shelf. Space the brads about 3 inches apart. Fit the upper shelf. Remove it and fasten to it the partition, with the brads driven through the shelf into the edge of the partition, placing the partition at the center of the shelf. Place the shelf and partition, and secure the shelf in the same manner as the lower shelf, having the partition close up to the end of the box. Set the partition vertically true and secure it with brads driven through the end of the box into its edge. Nail on the corner trim, placing one on the corner of each closet box. Make the door to fit between the corner trim. Make it ¼ inch shorter than the outside length of the box. Put the cleats on; the upper one just low enough to clear the upper shelf, and the lower one the same distance up from the bottom end. Lay the door on, having the top end even with the end of the box. Place the hinges about 15 inches apart and equal distance from the ends. Screw the knob on the door midway the height and 2 inches from the edge. A small screw-button may be placed on the leg opposite the knob to hold the door closed. Duplicate this with the other large box. Stand both closets on end, space apart, and put the top on, having the rear edge even with the face of the corner trim. Have the ends and front project equally, then nail securely to each closet. Cut away the back half of the lower end of the rear inside corner trim for a height of 6 inches from the bottom end of the closets, to receive the brace. Put the brace on and nail it in place. It will extend across the rear of the closets at the bottom, fitting into the recess made in the two inside corner trims, and its ends will butt against the outside corner strips, its rear face being even with the rear face of the corner trim. Place the small boxes which are to form the pigeonholes, and fasten them by nails driven from the inside of the box into the top of the desk, having their ends and rear faces even with the edges of the desk top. Fit and secure the shelves and partitions with small brads in the same manner as those for the closets. Put a small cleat 3/8 inch thick and 3/4 inch deep on the inner ends of each box, and cut the shelf to length and fasten with brads driven through near its ends into the cleats.

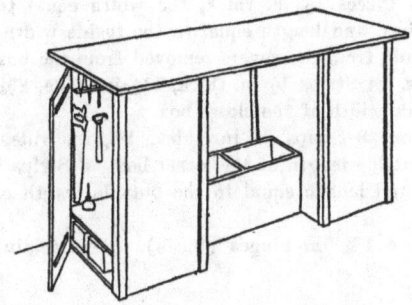

BOY'S WORK-TABLE
Illustration 80   *Figure 1*

Similar to the Teacher's Desk, without the upper compartments and having the closets open at the sides instead of in front; the waste box between, acting as a brace, makes a rear brace as in the Teacher's Desk unnecessary.

NOTE. The Kitchen Table is made the same as the Boy's Work-Table, except that the closets are provided with additional shelves and have no doors, and two shelves in the recess supplant the waste box between the closets.

Requirements:

Closets. 2 Rubber-shoe Boxes (about 13½ in. deep, 14½ in. wide, 27½ in. long).

Waste Receptacle. 1 Jam Box (about 11⅛ in. deep, 7⅝ in. wide, 18 in. long).

Bench Top. 1 Piece 1 in. thick, 6 in. wider than the outside width of the closet boxes, 6 in. longer than twice the outside depth of the closet boxes added to the outside length of the waste-receptacle box (2 boards wide).

Shelves. 4 Pieces ½ in. thick, the width equal to the inside depth of the box, and length equal to the inside width of the box.

Doors. Made from the covers removed from the boxes.

Door Cleats. 4 Strips ½ in. thick, 1½ in. wide, 2¾ in. shorter than the outside width of the closet box.

Corner Trim. 8 Strips ⅜ in. thick, 1⅜ in. wide, and length equal to the outside length of the closet box. 8 Strips ⅜ in. thick, 1¾ in. wide, and length equal to the outside length of the closet box.

Hardware. 4 1¾ in. hinges (butts). 2 porcelain pull-knobs. 2 buttons.

Construction:

Make the corner trim the length of the outside length of the closet box. Remove the covers. Nail the corner trim on both closet boxes and stand them on end on the floor 22½ inches apart, with their closed backs facing each other. Place the waste-wood receptacle on the floor between them, its open top facing up, and nail each end of it to one of the closets. The waste box should be in a central line with the closets. Clinch the nails and fit and nail the shelves in place, one shelf in the closet containing the long tools and three in the other closet, spaced apart as will be most convenient. Put the top on and nail it in place, allowing it to project 3 inches over the face of the doors and the same over the sides of the closets. Make and fit the doors, putting the cleats on the inside face at such heights as not to interfere with the shelves when the doors are closed. Hang the doors and screw on the pull-knobs and buttons.

BOX FURNITURE

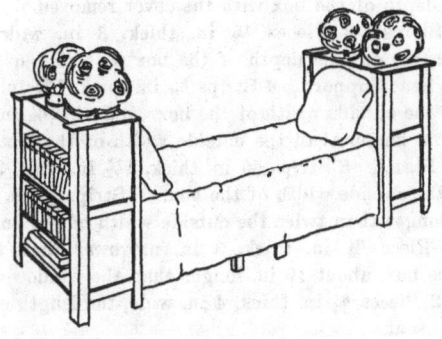

WINDOW-SEAT

Illustration 81 *Figures 1 and 2*

This practical Window-Seat is made by combining two Flower- and Plant-Stands having slots cut across in the back of each to receive the ends of a portable seat which is supported at its center by a box made similar to the Coal- or Paper-Box, without its cover, Illustration 16. As the individual pieces forming the window-seat merely support or rest upon each other, they may easily be assembled or removed as desired. The box support compartment makes a convenient receptacle for coverings and pillows when not in use and can be readily withdrawn, as the seat merely rests upon it.

Requirements:

Bodies. 4 Soap Boxes (about 10¾ in. deep, 14¼ in. wide, 20 in. long). 1 Box of the same width and depth, but 4 in. shorter, so that it will not project outside the edge of the seat.

Top Compartment Sides. 2 Pieces ½ in. thick, 6 in. wide, by the length of the box inside.

Arms. 4 Pieces ½ in. thick, 3 in. wide, by 3 in. longer than the outside depth of the box with the cover removed.

Facing Strips. 8 Pieces ½ in. thick, 3 in. wide, by 3 in. shorter than the outside depth of the box with the cover removed.

Legs for Seat Support. 4 Strips ⅜ in. thick, 1⅜ in. wide, 4 in. longer than the outside width of the box. 4 Strips ⅜ in. thick, 1¾ in. wide, 4 in. longer than the outside width of the box.

Legs for Stand. 8 Strips ½ in. thick, 1½ in. wide, 3 in. longer than twice the outside width of the box. 8 Strips ½ in. thick, 2 in. wide, 3 in. longer than twice the outside width of the box.

Seat. 1 Piece ¾ in. thick, 3 in. narrower than the outside length of the box, about 10 in. longer than the window-sill.

Cleats. 2 Pieces ¾ in. thick, 4 in. wide, the length equal to the width of the seat.

Construction:

For making the end supports, see description for constructing Flower- and Book-Stand, Illustration 53. In addition to this it will be necessary to cut a slot 1 inch high in the back of each stand, extending from leg to leg, and each end of the seat will pass through the slot and project about 3 inches inside, and will rest upon the

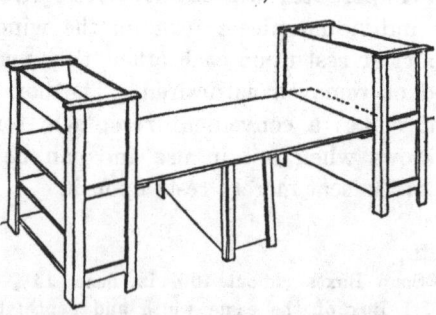

bottom of the upper compartment. The seat can be made of two boards held together by cleats nailed across them on their under side. Keep the nearest edge of cleat

3½ inches from the end of the seat. Drive the nails from the top of the seat through the cleats and clinch them well on the under side.

Remove the cover from the smaller box and make the legs. Nail a leg on each corner, keeping their top ends even with the top of the box. Turn the box upon its legs and place it under the seat to act as a center support.

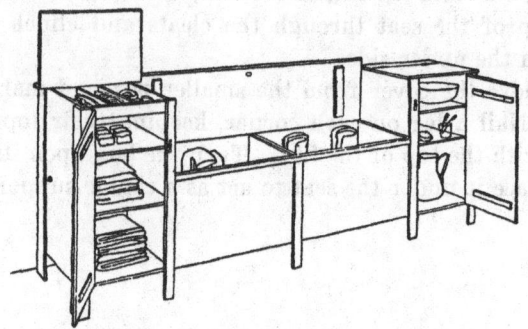

BEDROOM WINDOW-SEAT

Illustration 82   *Figures 1 and 2*

A combination of a window-seat, washstand, and underwear closet, the length of the seat compartment being made to suit the width of the window. The washstand is shown on the right and the underwear closet on the left, having a top compartment fitted to keep neckwear or handkerchiefs The seat boxes may contain shoes, extra bedding, or other articles, while toilet articles may be kept in the various compartments.

Requirements:

Closets. 2 Packing-boxes (about 14 in. deep, 21 in. wide, 34 in. long).

Seat Support. 2 Packing-boxes (about 12 in. deep, 14 in. wide, 22 in. long).

Closet Tops. 2 Pieces ½ in. thick, 2 in. wider than the outside depth of the closet boxes, 3 in. longer than the outside width of the closet boxes.

Seat. 1 Piece ⅝ in. thick, 1 in. wider than the outside width, and twice the length of the seat box.

Seat Cleats. 2 Pieces ½ in. thick, 3 in. wide, the length equal to the inside width of the box.

Shelves. 4 Pieces ½ in. thick, the width equal to the inside depth of the closet box, and length equal to the inside width of the box.

Partitions. 2 Strips ⅜ in. thick, 2 in. wide, ⅜ in. shorter than the inside depth of the box.

Top Compartment Front Face. 1 Strip ½ in. thick, 2 in. wide, and length equal to the inside width of the box.

Doors. Made from the covers of the closet boxes.

Door Cleats. 4 Strips ½ in. thick, 1½ in. wide, 4 in. shorter than the outside width of the closet boxes.

Corner Legs. 4 Strips ½ in. thick, 1½ in. wide, 4 in. longer than the outside length of the closet boxes. 4 Strips ½ in. thick, 2 in. wide, 4 in. longer than the outside length of the closet boxes.

Facing Strip Legs. 4 Strips ½ in. thick, 2 in. wide, 4 in. longer than the outside length of the closet boxes. 2 Strips ½ in. thick, 2 in. wide, 2 in. longer than the outside depth of the seat box with the cover removed.

Seat Facing Strip. 2 Strips ½ in. thick, 2 in. wide, 1 in. shorter than twice the outside length of the seat box.

Hardware. 8 1¾ in. brass hinges (butts) and screws. 3 2 in. brass hinges (butts) and screws. 2 brass pull-knobs. 2 brass buttons and screws.

Construction:

Make the corner legs 4 inches longer than the outside length of the larger or closet boxes. Remove the covers from all and one end from each of the closet boxes. The ends removed may be used for the lower shelf in each closet. Fit and nail the shelves in place in both closets, setting those in the washstand at the proper height to suit the pail, pitcher, and bowl, as in the Office Washstand. (See Illustration 39.) Set those in the other closet to suit the underclothing which they will contain. Or, if spaced as shown in the illustration, the height of the compartments, naming them from the bottom up, would be about 12 inches, 10 inches, 7 inches, and 2 inches. Stand one of the seat boxes on end and place the other one upon it endwise, with both open compartments facing the same way, and nail them together. Upon the end of the top one place one of the closets on its side, having the open end facing the same way and the closed end even with the bottom of the seat box. Match their edges and nail

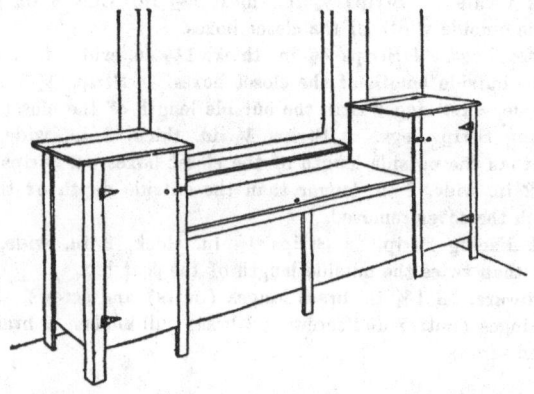

them together. Reverse them and join the other closet box in the same manner. Nail the four corner and four facing strip legs on the closets, front and rear, allowing the outside edge of the facing strip legs to project ½ inch over the outside face of the closets, having their upper ends even with the top of the closets. Place and nail the facing strips along each top side of the seat boxes, having the upper edge of the strips even with the top edges of the boxes. Put the seat facing strip legs on, front and rear, and turn the piece upon its legs. Place and nail the front face of the top compartment of the underwear closet and set in and nail the partitions. The hinged tops will be made in two pieces, the narrow piece of each being 4 inches wide. Nail one narrow piece on each closet, allowing it to project over the face of the legs 1 inch at the sides and rear. Hang the wide piece to this narrow one. Put the cleats on the doors, one 4 inches from each end. Fit and hang the doors and screw on the pull-knobs and the buttons.

Make and fit the seat, putting the cleats 6 inches from each end, allowing even space at each end of the cleat. The seat will not be hinged, and when closed the cleats should fit inside the boxes and hold the seat from side movement.

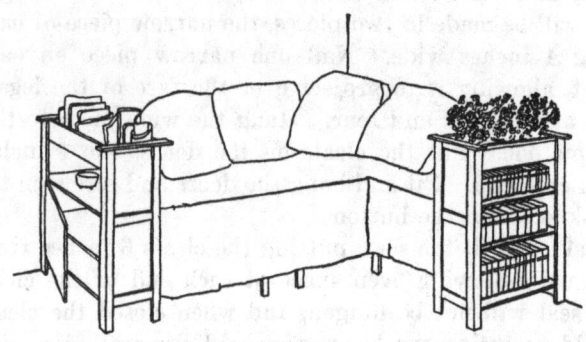

COLLEGE CORNER SEAT

Illustration 83   *Figures 1 and 2*

Requirements:

The same as for the Window-seat (Illustration 81), with the addition of two boxes supported on legs, as follows:

Ell Seat. 1 Soap Box (about 8¾ in. deep, 15½ in. wide, 20½ in. long).

End Support. 1 Candle Box (about 10¾ in. deep, 12½ in. wide, 16 in. long).

Legs. 8 Strips ⅜ in. thick, 1⅜ in. wide, 18¼ in. long. 8 Strips ⅜ in. thick, 1¾ in. wide, 18¼ in. long.

Seat Cover. 1 Piece ¾ in. thick, the width equal to the outside width of the ell seat box, and length equal to the outside length of the box.

Construction:

Make two Flower- and Book-Stands, as described in Illustration 53, and provide slot opening in one to receive the seat; also provide a seat support as described for the Window-seat. Make the legs 18¼ inches long. Remove the covers. Nail a leg on the corner of each box, allowing them to project below the bottom, having their other ends even with the open top end. Make a cover for the box which is to form the ell portion of the seat, putting a cleat near each end on the under side. This box will form the short or ell portion of the seat and will stand at a right angle to the long portion of the seat, with one flower-stand at its outer end. The cover of the box will form the seat and will not be hinged. The end of the long seat will be supported by a box placed under it in the corner.

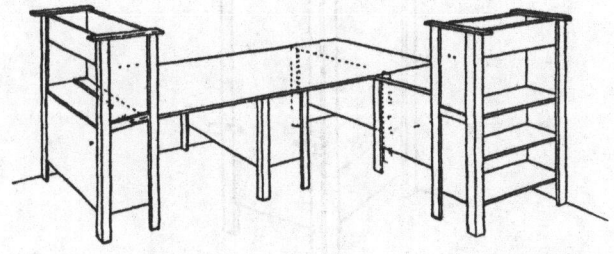

BOX FURNITURE

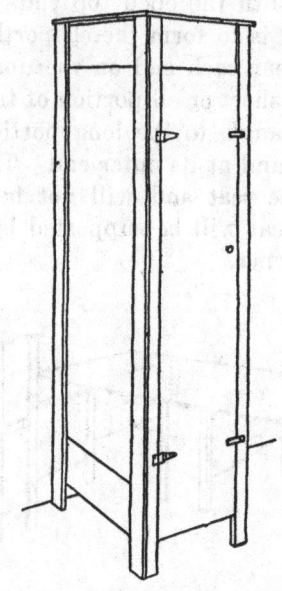

SINGLE WARDROBE

Illustration 84   *Figure 1*

This is made with the hat compartment door opening on the left.

Requirements:
Body. 2 Washing-powder Boxes (8¾ in. deep, 15¾ in. wide, 30 in. long). 1 Long Packing-box (15¾ in. deep, 30 in. wide, 6 ft. long).

Legs. 4 Strips ½ in. thick, 1¼ in. wide, by twice the outside depth of the small boxes and the outside length of the packing-box combined. 4 Strips ½ in. thick, 1¾ in. wide, by twice the outside depth of the small boxes and the outside length of the packing-box combined.

Cleats. 2 Strips ½ in. thick, 1½ in. wide, and 1 in. shorter than the width of the door.

Hardware. 2 porcelain pull-knobs. 2 4 in. tee hinges. 4 1½ in. butts and screws. 3 screws 1 in. long, to screw on buttons. 3 wooden buttons, for fastening doors.

False Top. 1 Piece ½ in. thick, 3 in. wider than the outside width and 3 in. longer than the outside length of the small boxes.

Construction:

Make the length of the legs twice the outside depth of the small boxes and the outside length of the packing-box combined.

Take one end out of one, and one side out of the other small box, and put the covers back on the boxes. Set one box flat on the floor, and stand the packing-box on end on top of it. If the packing-box is not the right size, it will have to be taken apart and its boards cut to the proper dimensions. When it is the same size in width and depth as the small box, nail the two boxes together, the openings on the same side, and clinch the nails. These two boxes make the compartments for clothes and for shoes.

Put the other small box on the floor. Set the packing-box, upside down, on top of it, having the opening of the small box at right angles with the opening of the packing-box. Nail the boxes together evenly, and turn the wardrobe right side up. The second small box makes the hat compartment. Nail the false top over the top of the hat compartment. It should project 1½ inches beyond each edge.

Nail the legs to the corners of the wardrobe. Their tops should reach to the false top, and they should extend

4 inches below the bottom. Be sure the legs are even, then stand the wardrobe upright on them.

Make the wardrobe door. Let it fit easily between the legs and extend from the bottom of the hat compartment down to the bottom of the shoe compartment. Nail the cleats on the door 8 inches from each end. Place the tee hinges 1 foot from each end and hang the door. Screw the knob in the middle, 2 inches from the outer edge. Screw the buttons on the legs 1 foot from each end of the door.

The side removed from the small box cut shorter will make a door for the hat compartment. Hang it from the top, as shown in Illustration 85, and put on a knob and button.

The clothes-hanger support inside the wardrobe is made of a broom handle $\frac{1}{2}$ inch shorter than the width of the clothes compartment. Make two blocks, 3 inches square and $\frac{3}{4}$ inch thick. Bore a hole the size of the broom handle through the middle of each block. Slip the broom handle through the blocks, and nail the blocks to the sides of the wardrobe 2 inches from the top. Many clothes-hangers may be hung upon this rod. The above description is for a man's wardrobe. The only difference, however, between that and the woman's wardrobe is in the height of the shoe compartment, which is 15 inches high instead of $8\frac{1}{4}$ inches. The increased height is obtained by removing the cover also from the lower small box and moving the lower end of the packing-box in about $6\frac{1}{4}$ inches.

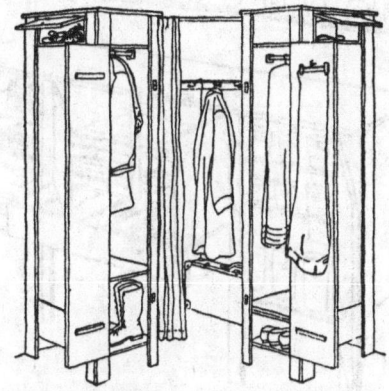

DOUBLE WARDROBE

Illustration 85 *Figure 1*

Make two Single Wardrobes, as per Illustration 84, and place them on the floor near one corner of the room. Fit a broom-handle bar between them at the top of the wardrobes. A curtain hung from this bar will make a convenient recess for hanging outdoor wraps in the corner between the two wardrobes.

The doors of the double wardrobe and of the hat compartments should be hung in such a manner as to open, one right and the other left hand, as shown in the illustration.

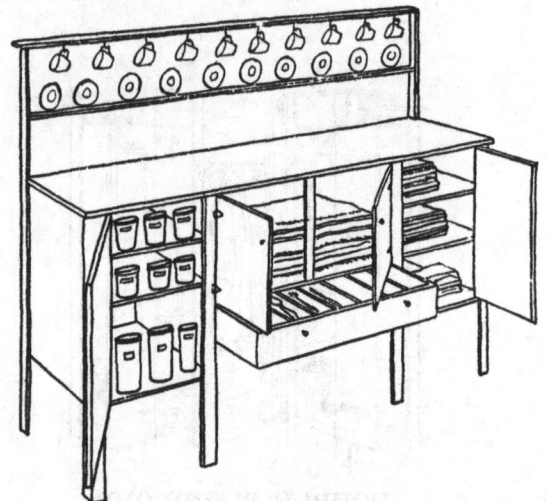

SPITZBERGEN SIDEBOARD

Illustration 86   *Figures 1 and 2*

Requirements:

Side Cupboards. 2 Dynamite Boxes (about 11 in. deep, 11 in. wide, 22 in. long).

Center Cupboard. 1 Carbonite Box (about 10 in. deep, 12 in. wide, 31 in. long).

Drawer. 1 Picture Box (about 5 in. deep, 10 in. wide, 31 in. long).

False Top. 1 Piece ½ in. thick, 1½ in. wider than the outside depth of the side cupboard box with the cover removed, and 2 in. longer than twice the outside width of the side cupboard box and the outside length of the center cupboard box added.

Recess Shelves. 2 Pieces ½ in. thick, ½ in. wider than the outside depth of the side cupboard, and the length equal to the outside length of the center cupboard box.

Cupboard Shelves. 4 Pieces ½ in. thick, width equal to the inside depth of the box, and length equal to the inside width of the box.

Doors. Made from the covers removed from the boxes.

Drawer Partitions. 9 Pieces ⅜ in. thick, width equal to the inside depth of the drawer box, and length equal to the inside width of the drawer box.

Corner Legs. 2 Strips ½ in. thick, 2 in. wide, 55 in. long.
              2 Strips ½ in. thick, 2½ in. wide, 55 in. long.
              2 Strips ½ in. thick, 2 in. wide, 35 in. long.
              2 Strips ½ in. thick, 2½ in. wide, 35 in. long.

Facing Strip Legs. 4 Strips ½ in. thick, 2½ in. wide, 35 in. long.

Back of Rack. 1 Piece ½ in. thick, 8 in. wide, 2 in. shorter than the false top.

Bottom of Rack. 1 Strip ½ in. thick, 3½ in. wide, 2 in. shorter than the false top.

Top of Rack. 1 Strip ½ in. thick, 2½ in. wide, 1 in. longer than the false top.

Center Cupboard Dividing Strip. 1 Strip ½ in. thick, 2½ in. wide, and length equal to the outside width of the box.

Hardware. 8 1¾ in. tee hinges and screws.
           6 brass pull-knobs.
           4 brass buttons and screws.
           10 brass screw-hooks.

Construction:

Make two legs 35 inches and two 55 inches long. Remove the covers from all the boxes. Fit and nail two shelves in each of the cupboard boxes, forming three equal compartments in each. Place one side cupboard on its side and set the center cupboard on its end upon it, having one side even with the end of the side cupboard and both open compartments facing the same way, with the edges even, and nail them together. Join the other side cupboard box to the other end of the center cupboard box in the same manner. Turn the cupboards upside down and set one recess shelf on the center cupboard and nail it. Upon this set the drawer box, and upon the drawer box place the other recess shelf and nail it. Allow both of the recess shelves to project ½ inch outside the front edges of the cupboards. Put on the corner and the facing strip legs, having their upper ends even with the top of the cupboards, their other ends projecting 13 inches below the bottom face of the side cupboards, and the recess edge of the facing strip legs even with the outside side face of the side cupboard. Stand the piece upon its legs and place and nail the top, allowing it to project ½ inch over the outside face of the legs at the ends and in front, having its back edge even with the outside face of the rear legs. It will be necessary to cut the rear corners of the top to allow one side of each rear leg to set in about 1 inch. Place the back of the rack across and between the rear projecting legs and nail it to their inside faces, having its upper edge even with the top of the legs. Put the top of the rack across on top of the legs on its flat side, having its rear edge even with the back edge of the legs. Set the rack bottom between the legs and under the lower edge of the rack back, having its rear edge against the inside face of the legs. Nail both the top and bottom of the rack to the edge of the rack back. The end of the top of the rack will project 1 inch over the outside face of the legs. Gouge a groove in the top face of the rack bottom, extending its entire length with the exception of two inches at each end. Have it ⅜ inch wide and ⅛ inch deep, and ¾ inch from the front edge, to prevent the saucers from sliding. Cut off the projecting corners at each end to an angle of 45 degrees, as the shelf will project 1 inch outside the front edge of the legs. Place the saucers in the rack and screw the hooks to the under side of the top for holding the cups, having them hang between the saucers. Fit and nail the center cupboard division strip in the center of the cupboard, having its outer face even with the front edge of the recess shelves. Fit and hang the doors and screw on the pull-knobs and the buttons. Fit and nail the partitions in the drawer, spacing them about 3 inches apart, or to suit the knives, forks, and spoons which they will contain.

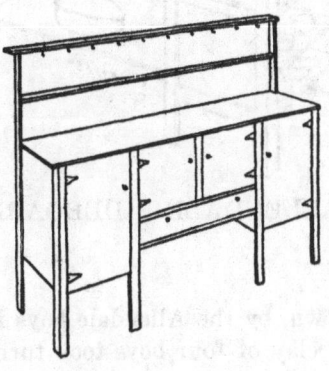

ALLENDALE SIDEBOARD

Illustration 87 *Figures 1 and 2*

Made as shown, by the Allendale boys in the Bradley Republic. A relay of four boys took turns in the "box factory" morning and afternoon. Their beaming faces when the work was completed showed the keen interest of all in creating "our sideboard," as the boys expressed it in a letter to me.

It consists of four boxes supported in pairs, with a recess containing shelves between. The recess is closed across the back. The rear legs carry up and support a cup-and-saucer rack. The space between the rack and the sideboard top is open. The compartments at each end are made alike.

BOX FURNITURE

Requirements:

Cupboards. 4 Canned-fruit Boxes (about 13 in. wide, 12½ in. deep, 18 in. long).

Recess Shelves. 3 Pieces ½ in. thick, the width equal to the outside length of the box, 24 in. long.

Inside Shelves. 2 Pieces ½ in. thick, the width ½ in. less than the inside depth of the box, and the length equal to the inside length of the box. 2 Pieces ½ in. thick, the width equal to the inside depth of the box, and the length equal to the inside length of the box.

Shelf Cleats. 8 Strips ⅜ in. thick, 1 in. wide, and the length equal to the inside depth of the box. 6 Strips ⅜ in. thick, 1½ in. wide, and the length equal to the outside length of the box.

Door Cleats. 4 Strips ⅜ in. thick, 1 in. wide, and the length 1 in. less than the inside width of the box.

Legs. 2 Strips ½ in. thick, 1½ in. wide, 8 in. longer than twice the outside width of the box. 2 Strips ½ in. thick, 2 in. wide, 8 in. longer than twice the outside width of the box. 2 Strips ½ in. thick, 1½ in. wide, 30 in. longer than twice the outside width of the box. 2 Strips ½ in. thick, 2 in. wide, 30 in. longer than twice the outside width of the box.

Back of Rack. 1 Strip ½ in. thick, 6 in. wide, 24 in. longer than twice the outside depth of the box.

Top of Rack. 1 Strip ½ in. thick, 2½ in. wide, 27 in. longer than twice the outside depth of the box.

Bottom of Rack. 1 Strip ½ in. thick, 2½ in. wide, 24 in. longer than twice the outside depth of the box.

Recess Back. 1 Piece ½ in. thick, the width twice the outside width of the box, 30 in. long.

Top. 1 Piece ½ in. thick, 2 in. wider than the outside length of the box, 27 in. longer than twice the outside width of the box.

Facing Strips. 4 Strips ½ in. thick, 2 in. wide, 8 in. longer than twice the outside width of the box. 4 Strips ½ in. thick, 2 in. wide, and the length 2½ in. less than the outside depth of the box.

Hardware. 4 1¼ in. hinges (butts) and screws. 2 pull-knobs. 9 brass hooks.

Construction:

Make the legs, two 8 inches and two 30 inches longer than twice the outside width of the box. Remove the covers. Lay one box on its side and place another box upon it sidewise, with both open sides facing alike. Match their edges and nail them together, driving the nails from the inside of the top box, and clinch them in the lower box. Nail the cleats on the inside ends of each box and fit the shelves in. (They need not be fastened.) The shelf in the upper box will be ½ inch less in width than the lower ones, to allow the door to close without the door cleats striking the shelf. Turn the boxes end up and put on the front corner leg, also the long facing strip leg, allowing its edge to project half over the recess to hide the ends of the recess shelf cleats. Nail the short facing strips between them, the middle one directly over the joint of both boxes, the upper edge of the top one even with the upper edge of the top of the box, and the lower edge of the bottom one even with the lower edge of the bottom of the box. Reverse the position of the boxes and put on the extended rear leg, keeping it the same distance below the lower box, so the cupboard will stand level. Fit the door between the legs, having the outer face of both the door and legs even. Put the cleats on the inside face of the door and hang it. Do the same with the other two boxes. They are to be made right- and left-handed regarding the position of the legs and the hanging of the door. Set both pairs of compartments upon their legs, 24 inches apart as shown, and fit and nail on the top, allowing it to project 1 inch at the ends and in front over the outside face of the legs, the rear edge being even with

BOX FURNITURE

the outside face of the rear legs. It will be necessary to cut out both rear corners of the top to allow the legs to set in. Put on the recess shelf cleats, keeping the lower edge of the bottom ones even with the lower side of the bottom box, and those above at such heights as will be best adapted for the articles to be placed on them. Fit in the shelves and nail their ends to the cleats. Nail the 6-inch-wide back for rack across the rear inside face of the top of the extended legs, and put on the top and bottom strips. Gouge or plane a groove in the bottom of the rack $\frac{3}{8}$ inch wide, $\frac{1}{8}$ inch deep, and $\frac{1}{2}$ inch back from the front edge, and cut off the projecting corners at each end to an angle of 45 degrees, as the shelf will project 1 inch outside the front edge of the legs. Allow the strip to butt against the legs at the back below the rack back, to which it should be nailed. Nail through the legs into the ends of the strip. Put the recess back on, which will extend from the under side of the top to the lower edge of the lower shelf cleats. Each end will lap about 3 inches on the cupboards. Arrange the saucers in the rack, and screw a hook directly below each one for holding the cups.

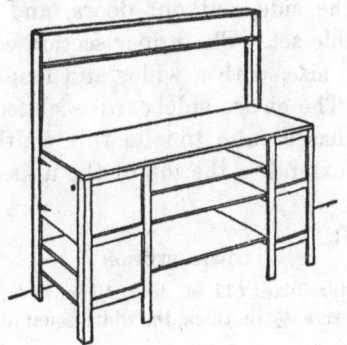

242 BOX FURNITURE

COPENHAGEN SIDEBOARD
Illustration 88   *Figures 1 and 2*

Made of seven boxes, the four larger ones, forming the lower section, being alike. The two end compartments are open at the side, without doors, and afford ample space for a table set. The upper section consists of two boxes of equal size, with a wider and longer box set between them. The entire sideboard is closed at the back. Each section has a false top its full width and length. The rear legs extend to the top of the upper section.

Requirements:
LOWER SECTION
Body. 4 Butter Boxes (11 in. deep, 16 in. wide, 22 in. long).
Shelves. 4 Pieces ½ in. thick, the width equal to the inside depth

of the box, and the length equal to the inside width of the box. 2 Pieces ½ in. thick, the width equal to the inside depth of the box, and the length equal to the inside width of the box.

Shelf Cleats. 8 Strips ½ in. thick, 1 in. wide, and the length equal to the inside depth of the box. 4 Strips ½ in. thick, 1 in. wide, and the length equal to the inside depth of the box.

Doors. Made from the covers.

Door Cleats. 4 Strips ½ in. thick, 1 in. wide, 1 in. shorter than the width of the door.

Facing Strips. 3 Strips ½ in. thick, 2 in. wide, 11 in. longer than the outside length of the box.

Legs. 2 Strips ½ in. thick, 1½ in. wide, 11 in. longer than the combined heights of both sections and the thickness of the top added. 2 Strips ½ in. thick, 2 in. wide, 11 in. longer than the combined heights of both sections and the thickness of the top added. 2 Strips ½ in. thick, 1½ in. wide, 11 in. longer than the outside length of the box. 2 Strips ½ in. thick, 2 in. wide, 11 in. longer than the outside length of the box.

Hardware. 4 tee hinges and screws. 2 pull-knobs. 2 buttons.

Top. 1 Piece ¾ in. thick, 1½ in. wider than the outside depth of the box, 2 in. longer than four times the outside width of the box.

UPPER SECTION

Body. 2 Dried-fruit Boxes (3½ in. deep, 11 in. wide, 14 in. long). 1 Dried-fruit Box (3½ in. deep, 14 in. wide, 32 in. long).

Shelves. 4 Pieces ⅜ in. thick, the width equal to the inside depth of the box, and the length equal to the inside width of the small box. 1 Piece ⅜ in. thick, the width equal to the inside depth of the box, and the length equal to the inside length of the large box.

Doors. Made from the covers.

Facing Strips. 4 Strips ⅜ in. thick, 1½ in. wide, and the length equal to the outside length of the small box.

Top. 1 Piece ½ in. thick, 1 in. wider than the outside depth of the box, 2 in. longer than the outside length of the large and twice the outside width of the small box.

Hardware. 4 1¼ in. brass butts and screws. 2 pull-knobs. 2 brass buttons.

Construction:

LOWER SECTION

Make the legs—two, 11 inches longer than the outside length of the boxes; two, 11 inches longer than the combined outside length of both the upper and lower boxes and the thickness of the top added.

Remove the covers from two of the boxes and fit and nail the shelves in, one shelf being 8 inches from one end and the other 5 inches from the other end, measured inside. Nail them through the sides into the ends of the shelves. Lay one box on its side and place the other on its side upon it. Match the edges and nail them together through their abutting sides, and clinch the points of the nails.

Remove one side from each of the other two boxes, and fit and nail a shelf in each midway its length. Place one of these boxes on its side upon the other two, with the open side up, and nail to the one below it as before, having the outside face even with the edges of the open compartments of the others. Invert them and place and nail the last box in the same manner. Turn them flat side down, the open side of the middle compartments facing up, and put on both the corner and the facing strip legs, the front legs having their upper ends even with the top end of the boxes, allowing all their lower ends to project 11 inches below the other end. Nail the cleats to the inside face of the doors. Fit and hang the doors and turn the piece face down, and put on the rear legs, one at each corner, allowing their lower ends to project 11 inches. (The end boxes will project the thickness of the covers beyond the backs of the middle boxes.) Turn the sideboard upon its legs and nail on the top, having its rear edge even with the back face of the rear legs, allowing it to project ½ inch over the outer face of the legs in front and at the ends. It will be necessary to cut the rear corners of the top and let the legs in about an inch.

TOP SECTION

Remove the covers from the small boxes and fit and nail the shelves in place, having one shelf 4 inches from the inside face of one end and the other shelf 3 inches from the inside face of the other end. Before nailing in the shelves, however, bore five holes in each shelf about 1 inch from the edge, the holes being just large enough in diameter for the handles of the spoons to pass through. Fit and nail the shelf in the larger box, placing the shelf midway the width of the box. Place the larger box on end, and upon it place one of the small boxes laid on its side, the open compartments all facing the same way. Nail the other small box to the other end, matching the edges of all of them before nailing together. Place this section upon the lower section between the rear legs and nail the legs to it. Nail on the facing strips, keeping the outer edge of the end ones even with the end face and the inner edges of the inner ones even with the inside end face of the middle compartment. Nail on the top, having it even with the rear face of the legs and allowing it to project ½ inch over the outside face of the legs at the ends and front. Fit and hang the doors, having their outer faces even with the outer face of the facing strips.

Make a groove, ¼ inch wide and ⅛ inch deep, the entire length of the shelf, and a similar groove in the bottom of the cup-and-saucer compartment, 2 inches back from the front edge, to keep the saucers from sliding forward. Place the saucers in position and screw hooks to the under side of the shelf and to the top of the upper compartment, in line with the center of the saucers, on which to hang the cups. Screw on the pull-knobs and buttons.

CHAPTER XII

THE SAME PRINCIPLES AS CHAPTER XI WITH THE ADDITION OF FRAMEWORK

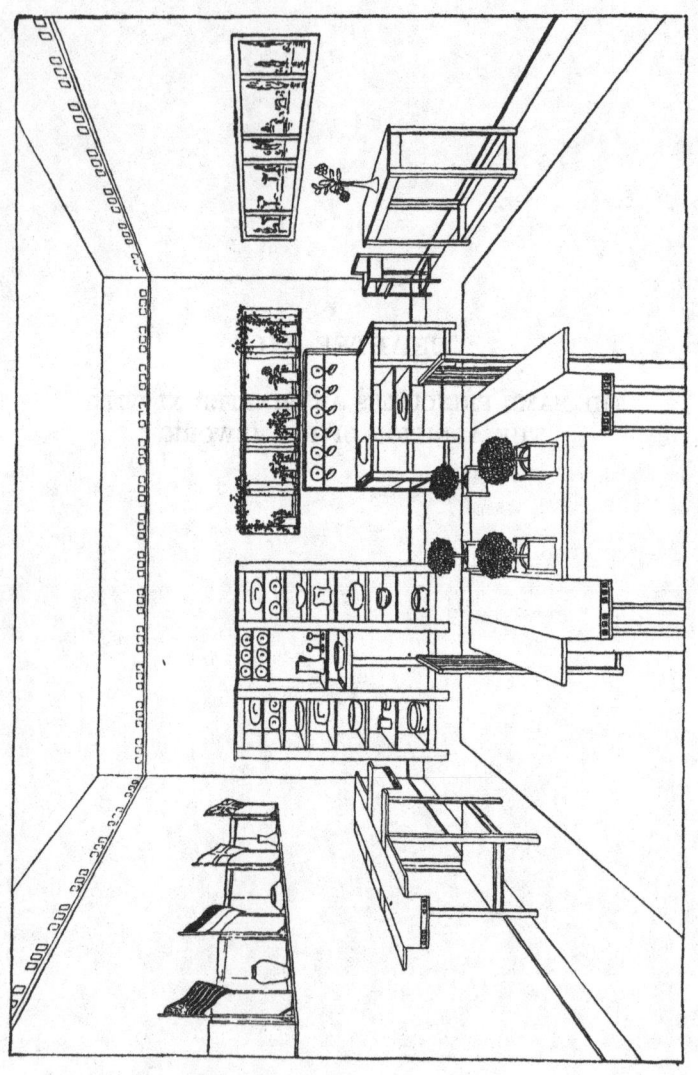

The Dining-Room

FLAG WALL RACK   CHINA CLOSET
ALLENDALE SIDEBOARD
GREEK-CROSS TABLE   MINIATURE PLANT-BOXES
VINE VASES
ROLLING SOILED-DISH STAND   BABY'S HIGH CHAIR
PICTURE FRAME NO. 2

Color Scheme:
    Flemish oak.
    Soft green.

Woodwork:
    Flemish oak.

Furniture:
    Flemish oak.

Walls:
    Soft green.

Drop Ceiling:
    Light green, with motif stenciled in moss green.

Hangings and Table-covers:
    Russian crash, with motif appliquéd or stenciled in same color as walls.

Curtains:
    White.

China:
    White.

Pottery:
    Green.

Floor:
    Stained same color as furniture.

Plants:
    Growing ivy and plants with crimson blossoms the same color as the flags; yellow or old-rose flowers if flags are not used.

CHAPTER XII

Illustration 89
CORNER WASHSTAND

One box placed top side up, one end removed and circle cut in cover. One box placed on end, one side removed and hinged as door. Shelf, legs, and trim added.

Illustration 90
COMBINATION WASHSTAND AND WARDROBE

A combination of Illustration 89 and Illustration 84.

Illustration 91
"SHAVINGETTE"

One box placed on end, cover removed and hinged as door. Shelves, legs, mirror, and false top added.

Illustration 92
TRIPLE-MIRROR DRESSING-TABLE

Two boxes placed on end, one side of each removed and hinged as doors. One box placed top side up, cover removed. Shelves, legs, mirror posts, mirrors, and false top added.

Illustration 93
DRESSING-TABLE

Five boxes placed top side up, one end removed from each and hinged as door. One box placed top side up, cover removed and hinged as door. Two boxes placed on end, covers removed. Shelves, legs, mirror, and false top added.

Illustration 94
WASHSTAND AND DRESSER

Four boxes placed top side up, one end of each removed. One box placed on end, cover removed. Four boxes placed on end, covers of all removed and covers of two hinged as doors. Shelves, legs, doors, and false top added.

Illustration 95
CHILD'S WASHSTAND AND DRESSER

Four boxes placed top side up, one end of each removed. One box placed on end, cover removed. Two boxes placed on end, covers removed. Legs, doors, and false top added.

Illustration 96
CHINA CLOSET

Three boxes placed on end, covers removed. Shelves, doors, legs, and false top added.

Illustration 97
HALL STAND

Three boxes placed top side up, each one cut down. Three boxes placed on end, covers and one end removed. One box placed on end, cover removed. One box placed top side up, cover removed. Legs, facing strips, framework, and mirror added.

Illustration 98
BOY'S DELIGHT

Eight boxes placed top side up, covers removed from all and two hinged as lids. Legs and corner trim added.

Illustration 99
CLUB-ROOM CORNER SEAT

Two packing-boxes placed top side up, covers removed and hinged as lids. Legs added. Six (small) butter boxes placed at end of packing-boxes, one upon the other, top side up, one side removed from four and covers from all. Two silk boxes placed on end at side of butter boxes, covers removed. Shelves and false top added. Two very long boxes made to fit space at other side of butter boxes. Shelf added. Wall protector made from parts of ten silk boxes nailed to back of packing-boxes.

Illustration 100
COMBINATION DESK, READING-TABLE, AND BOOKCASE

Eight boxes placed on end. Covers of six removed, two hinged as doors. One side of two removed. One box placed top side up, cover removed. Shelves, legs, trims, lamps, and false top added.

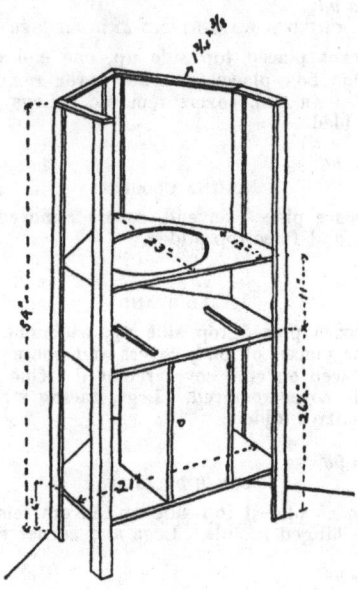

CORNER WASHSTAND
Illustration 89 *Figure 1*

This provides a towel cupboard below, with space on either side for a pitcher of hot and cold water.

Above this is a compartment wide enough to place a foot-tub. This compartment is made from practically a square box, with the two rear corners cut off at an angle of 45 degrees, and a circular opening made in the top the size of the wash-bowl. The foot-tub may be used for the morning bath, and also as a receptacle for waste water.

The upper framework (or projecting legs) serves as a splasher and towel rack.

A white enameled oil-cloth is nailed over the top and hangs down over the front, covering the open compartment.

Requirements:

Body. 1 Shoe Box (about 11 in. deep, 23 in. wide, 21 in. long).

Towel Closet. 1 Condensed-milk Box (about 7¼ in. deep, 13 in. wide, 19¾ in. long).

Shelf. 1 Piece ½ in. thick, 21 in. wide, 12 in. side and 23 in. center length.

Shelf Cleats. 2 Pieces ⅝ in. thick, 1⅜ in. wide, 21 in. long.

Door. Made from the end removed from the closet box.

Legs. 5 Strips ⅜ in. thick, 1⅜ in. wide, 54 in. long. 5 Strips ⅜ in. thick, 1¼ in. wide, 54 in. long.

Top Facing Strips. 2 Strips ⅜ in. thick, 1⅜ in. wide, about 14 in. long. 2 Strips ⅜ in. thick, 1⅜ in. wide, about 17 in. long.

Waterproof Cover and Flap Curtain. 1 square yard of white enameled oil-cloth.

Hardware. 2 1½ in. brass hinges (butts) and screws. 1 porcelain pull-knob. 1 brass button.

Construction:

Make the legs 54 inches long. Remove both sides from the box. From the open side which is to be the front, measure 12 inches back on each end, and from these points cut off (at an angle of 45 degrees) the rear corners of the box. Make side pieces for the angle openings thus made and nail them in. The compartment will be open in front only. Cut a circular opening 9 inches in diameter in the top in the center of the width, the edge of the opening being about 3 inches from the front of the box. Nail on the legs, allowing them to project 26½ inches below the bottom face of the box. Remove one side from the closet box. Turn the piece bottom up, resting on the top end of the legs, and set the closet box in place and nail it. Make the shelf the same shape as the body box and place on top of closet and nail the legs to its edges, and nail the shelf to the closet. Reverse the stand, turning it upon its legs. Cut and fit the top facing strips and nail them to the projecting leg tops. Fit and hang the door and screw on the pull-knob and the button. Cover the top of the stand with the enameled cloth and fit it around the opening as described for the Office Washstand, Illustration 39. In cutting the cloth, arrange to have it fall over the top in front and hang down about 11 inches, thus forming a flap curtain the full width between the front legs.

BOX FURNITURE 255

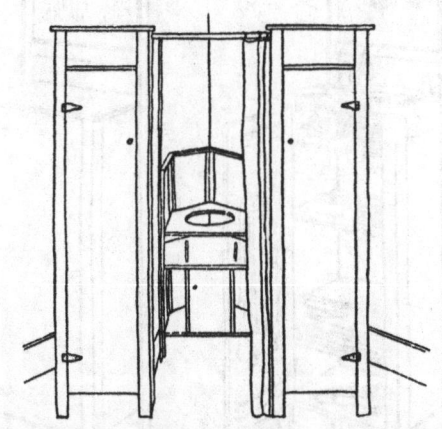

COMBINATION WASHSTAND AND WARDROBE

Illustration 90 *Figure 1*

On either side and a little forward of the Corner Washstand (Illustration 89) are placed two Single Wardrobes (Illustration 84), both facing from the Washstand, with ample space between them to permit one to bathe behind a hanging curtain placed between and at the front of the wardrobes, which, when drawn, incloses the space.

256   BOX FURNITURE

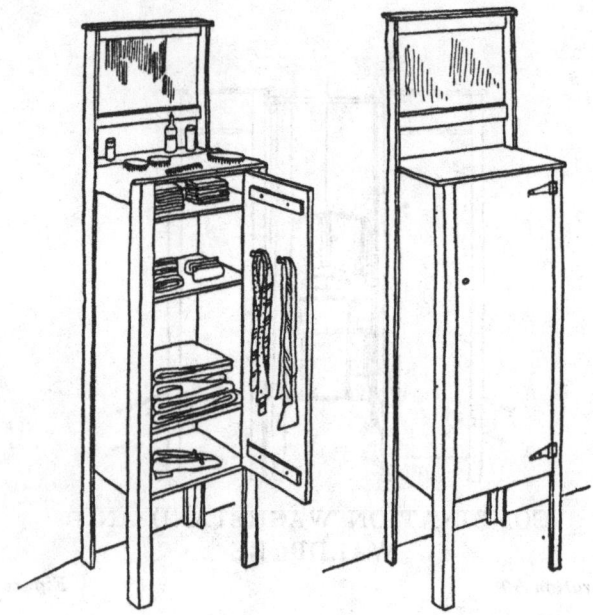

"SHAVINGETTE"

Illustration 91   *Figures 1 and 2*

Requirements:

Body. 1 Carpet-sweeper Box (11¾ in. deep, 15½ in. wide, 55½ in. long·cut down to 40 in. long).

Top. 1 Piece ½ in. thick, 1¼ in. wider and 2½ in. longer than the outside size of the end of the box.

Shelves. 3 Pieces ½ in. thick, by the depth and the width of the inside of the box.

Door. Made from the cover of the box.

Door Cleats. 2 Strips ½ in. thick, 2 in. wide, 5 in. shorter than the outside width of the box.

BOX FURNITURE

Mirror Strips. 2 Strips ⅜ in. thick, 1¾ in. wide, and the length equal to the outside width of the box.

Top Mirror Strip. 1 Piece ⅜ in. thick, 1¾ in. wide, 3 in. longer than the outside width of the box.

Legs. 2 Strips ⅜ in. thick, 1⅜ in. wide, 66 in. long. 2 Strips ⅜ in. thick, 1¾ in. wide, 66 in. long. 2 Strips ⅜ in. thick, 1⅜ in. wide, 50 in. long. 2 Strips ⅜ in. thick, 1¾ in. wide, 50 in. long.

Mirror. 10½ in. wide, and the length equal to the outside width of the box.

Hardware. 2 4 in. tee hinges and screws. 1 porcelain pull-knob. 1 button.

Construction:

Make two legs 50 inches and two legs 66 inches long. Remove the cover. Fit in and fasten the shelves at suitable heights. Nail the two short legs on, keeping their ends at one end of the box even with the outside face, allowing them to project about 10 inches over the other end of the box. Turn the box over and nail on the long legs in such a manner that all four legs will project equally at one end, and the last two legs will then project about 16 inches at the other end, forming a frame in which to fasten the mirror. Stand the box upon its legs and fit and nail on the top, allowing it to project ¾ inch over the outside face of the legs in front and at both ends, keeping the rear edge even with the outside face of the rear legs. It will be necessary to cut the top slightly on each side so as to fit it around the rear legs. Cut a rabbet ¼ inch wide, as deep as the thickness of the mirror glass, on one edge of each strip, thus:

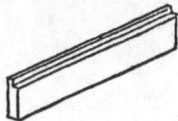

Nail one strip on the inside face of the rear leg, keeping the rabbeted edge at the top and in the rear. The bottom edge of this strip should be 2 inches above the top of the "Shavingette." Set the mirror between the rear projecting legs, with its lower edge in the rabbet and its rear face against the inner face of the rear legs. Place the other mirror strip across the top, with the top edge of the glass in the rabbet, and the top edge of the strip even with the upper ends of the legs. Place the top mirror strip across the top of the legs on its flat side, keeping its back edge even with the rear outside face of the legs, each end projecting 1 inch over the outside face of the leg. Put the cleats on the door and fit and hang it. Screw on the pull-knob and the button.

BOX FURNITURE 259

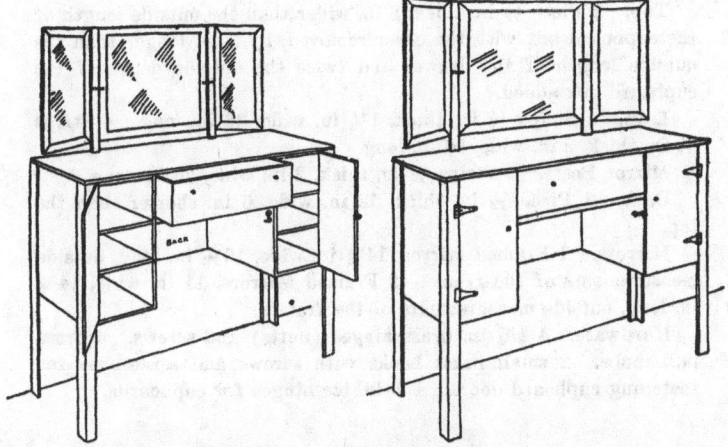

TRIPLE-MIRROR DRESSING-TABLE
Illustration 92 *Figures 1, 2, and 3*

The recess is made of sufficient width and height to receive the Dressing-table Chair when it is not in use.

Requirements:
Drawer. 1 Condensed-milk Box (about 7¼ in. deep, 13 in. wide, 19¾ in. long).

Cupboards. 2 Soap Boxes (about 11¾ in. deep, 14¼ in. wide, 20 in. long).

Recess Shelf. 1 Piece ½ in. thick, the width equal to the outside width of the cupboard box, and the length equal to the outside length of the drawer box.

Cupboard Shelves. 4 Pieces ½ in. thick, the width equal to the inside width of the box, and the length equal to the inside depth of the box.

Doors. 2 Pieces ½ in. thick, 1½ in. narrower than the outside depth of the box, and the length equal to the outside length of the box.

Top. 1 Piece ½ in. thick, 2 in. wider than the outside length of the cupboard box with the cover removed, by 3 in. longer than the outside length of the drawer and twice the outside depth of the cupboard box added.

Legs. 4 Strips ½ in. thick, 1½ in. wide, 36 in. long. 4 Strips ½ in. thick, 2 in. wide, 36 in. long.

Mirror Posts. 2 Strips ¾ in. thick, 2 in. wide, 26 in. long.

Back. 1 Piece ½ in. thick, 12 in. wide, 6 in. shorter than the top.

Mirrors. 1 Framed Mirror, 14¾ in. wide, 19½ in. long, outside measurements of the frame. 2 Framed Mirrors, 11 in. wide, 14¾ in. long, outside measurements of the frames.

Hardware. 4 1¾ in. brass hinges (butts) and screws. 4 brass pull-knobs. 2 small brass hooks with screws and screw-eyes for fastening cupboard doors. 4 3 in. tee hinges for cupboards.

Construction:

Make the corner legs 36 inches long. Remove one end from each of the cupboard boxes. Place and nail the shelves in each, and set them both on their sides, spaced apart the length of the drawer box. Place and nail the top to them, allowing it to project ½ inch at the rear and 1½ inches at the ends and in front. Reverse and remove the cover from the drawer box, and set it upside down between the cupboards. Place the recess shelf upon the drawer, match the edges, and nail it securely in place. Nail the legs on and place the back between the rear legs, having its lower edge even with the bottom of the cupboards, with its outer face even with the outer face of the legs, and nail it to the cupboards, then stand the table upon its legs. Place the front face of the drawer even with the front face of the cupboards, and nail a strip or block on the shelf behind the drawer to prevent its pushing in too far. The block or strip can be put on through the opening in the rear. Put the mirror posts on the rear face of the cupboards, their lower ends resting on the top edge of the back, having their inner side edges even with the side faces of the cupboards. It will be necessary to cut ½ inch by the width of the post out of the top for each post to set in. The post will stand about 17½ inches above the top of the table. Midway the height of the large mirror, bore a hole 3/16 inch in diameter and 1 inch deep in the ends of the mirror frame and through both posts, as shown by dotted lines in the illustration. Put a stout wire nail 3 inches long through the holes in each post, with the point end in the mirror frame, for the large mirror to swing on. Hang the side mirrors to the posts with four of the brass butts.

Home-made mirror frames may be made by using the grooved edge of a board ¾ inch thick and 2 inches wide. Miter the corners and nail or glue them with hot glue. Put three sides together, slip the glass in, and secure the other side.

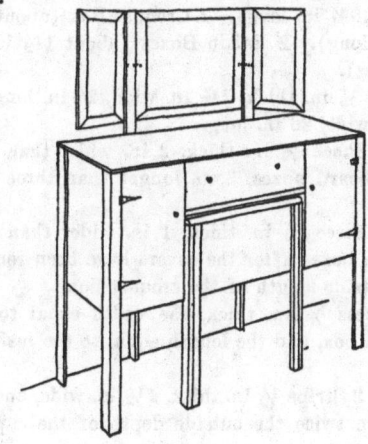

BOX FURNITURE

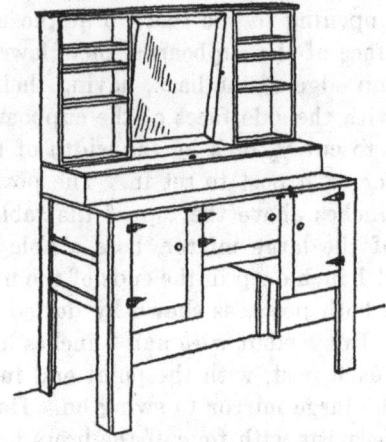

DRESSING-TABLE

Illustration 93 *Figures 1 and 2*

Requirements:

Cupboards and Body. 5 Condensed-milk Boxes (about 7¼ in. deep, 13 in. wide, 19¾ in. long). 1 Croquet Box (about 6 in. deep, 7 in. wide, 40 in. long). 2 Raisin Boxes (about 1½ in. deep, 9½ in. wide, 20 in. long).

Legs. 4 Strips ½ in. thick, 1½ in. wide, 26 in. long. 4 Strips ½ in. thick, 2 in. wide, 26 in. long.

Lower Top. 1 Piece ½ in. thick, 2 in. wider than the outside length of the cupboard boxes, 3 in. longer than three times their outside width.

Upper Top. 1 Piece ½ in. thick, 1 in. wider than the outside depth of the raisin boxes after the covers have been removed, 2 in. longer than the outside length of the croquet box.

Shelves. 6 Pieces ⅝ in. thick, the width equal to the inside depth of the raisin box, and the length equal to the inside width of the raisin box.

Facing Strips. 2 Strips ½ in. thick, 1½ in. wide, and the length 1½ in. longer than twice the outside depth of the cupboard box.

2 Strips ½ in. thick, 1½ in. wide, 2¼ in. shorter than the outside width of the box.

Mirror. 1 Framed Mirror, about 16 in. by 20 in. outside.

Hardware. 6 1½ in. butts and screws. 3 small pull-knobs. 3 brass buttons.

Construction:

LOWER SECTION

Make the legs 26 inches long. Remove the ends only from the five boxes. Set two boxes on their sides, one upon the other; match their edges and nail them together. Do the same with the third box, and have all their open ends facing the same way. Lay all three boxes flat side down on the floor and place the two remaining boxes, top side up, one upon each end box of the three, with all open ends facing the same way. Match their edges and nail them to the boxes beneath them. Turn them completely over upon the two last-added boxes. Fit and nail on the top, allowing it to project 1½ inches at the ends and in front and ½ inch at the back edge. Reverse the section and nail on the legs. Fit and nail on the facing strips, keeping those edges of the vertical strips which face each other even with the inside end face of the middle cupboard, allowing the strip to project slightly over the pair of compartments on each side. Have the upper edge of the horizontal strips even with the bottom of the lower compartment. Fit and hang the doors, screw on the knobs and buttons, and turn the section upon its legs.

UPPER SECTION

Place the croquet box on top of the section. Set the back of the box even with the back edge of the top, and nail it to the lower section, driving the nails inside the box, through the bottom, into the top of the lower section. Fit and nail the shelves in the raisin boxes.

The lid of the croquet box does not open the full width of its cover, but is hinged to a strip of the cover about 2 inches wide nailed across the top at the rear. Place the raisin boxes on end upon this strip, one at each end of the croquet box, having the outside side face even with the end of this box. Place the upper top across the top of the boxes and nail it to them, allowing it to project 1 inch at each end and in front, keeping the rear edge even with the rear face of the boxes.

Secure a piece of mirror glass and make a frame for it of strips 1 inch thick and 2 inches wide. Groove the strips with a grooving-plane to receive the glass, and miter and nail the corners together. The mirror frame is hung on two screws, one on each side, screwed through the sides of the raisin boxes into the mirror frame at a point midway of its height.

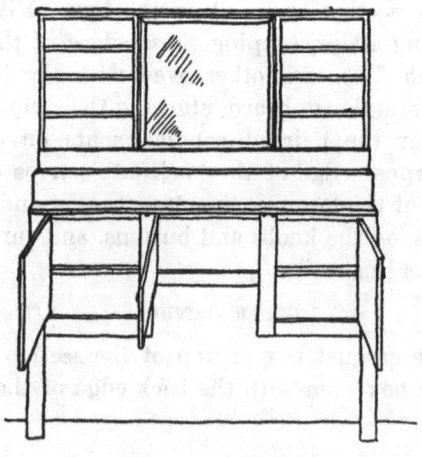

WASHSTAND AND DRESSER
Illustration 94 *Figures 1 and 2*

Provides space for toilet articles, underwear, ties, men's furnishings, shaving materials, photographs, and knickknacks.

This piece was made to meet a need in the far North, where the small accommodations required an article that would contain all the necessary toilet outfit and accessories needed by a man. The space below the mirror is open and has two broom-handle supports across it. A splasher hangs from the lower support and towels hang upon the upper one.

Requirements:

Lower Cupboards. 4 Condensed-milk Boxes (about 7¼ in. deep, 13 in. wide, 19¾ in. long).

Middle Compartment. 1 Small Packing-box (about 14½ in. deep, 20 in. wide, 21 in. long).

Upper Cupboard. 4 India-relish Boxes (7¼ in. deep, 12¼ in. wide, 16¾ in. long).

Shelves. 4 Pieces ½ in. thick, the width equal to the depth of the box, and the length equal to the width of the box.

Lower Top. 1 Piece ½ in. thick, 1½ in. wider than the length of the lower cupboard box by 2 in. longer than the packing-box and twice the width of the lower cupboard box combined.

Upper Top. 1 Piece ½ in. thick, 1 in. wider than the outside depth of the box, 2 in. longer than the packing-box and twice the width of the lower cupboard box combined.

Doors. 2 Pieces ½ in. thick, 2 in. narrower than the outside width of the cupboard box, and the length twice the outside depth of the cupboard box.

Facing Strips. 4 Strips ⅜ in. thick, 1¼ in. wide, and the length twice the outside length of the upper compartment box. 4 Strips ½ in. thick, 2 in. wide, 12 in. longer than twice the outside depth of the lower cupboard boxes. 4 Strips ½ in. thick, 2 in. wide, and the length 3 in. shorter than the lower cupboard boxes. 8 Strips ½ in. thick, 2 in. wide, 1½ in. shorter than the depth of the upper compartment boxes.

Legs. 2 Strips ½ in. thick, 1½ in. wide, 12 in. longer than twice the outside depth of the lower cupboard boxes. 2 Strips ½ in. thick, 2 in. wide, 12 in. longer than twice the outside depth of the lower cupboard boxes. 2 Strips ½ in. thick, 1½ in. wide, 12½ in. longer than twice the outside length of the upper compartment box and twice the outside depth of the lower cupboard boxes combined. 2 Strips ½ in. thick, 2 in. wide, 12½ in. longer than twice the outside length of the upper compartment box and twice the outside depth of the lower cupboard boxes combined.

Supports. 3 Broom Handles.

Hardware. 4 brass buttons. 4 hinges, 1¼ in. (butts). 4 pull-knobs. 2 hooks. 4 1¾ in. tee hinges.

Mirror. 1 Mirror.

Construction:

Make the legs, two 12 inches longer than twice the outside depth of the lower cupboard boxes, and two 12½ inches longer than twice the outside depth of the lower cupboard boxes and twice the outside length of the upper boxes combined. Remove the ends from the four lower cupboard boxes and the cover from the packing-box. Lay two lower cupboard boxes on their sides one upon the other, and nail together through the abutting sides. Do the same with the other two lower cupboard boxes. Make the packing-box the same width as the depth of a pair of the lower cupboard boxes. Place the packing-box on its end and set a pair of the lower cupboard boxes on their sides upon it. Match their edges and nail together. Join the other pair to the other end of the packing-box in the same manner, having all the openings facing alike. Turn them all over so the openings will all face up, and put on the corner legs and the facing strip legs. Reverse, having the openings down, and nail on the rear legs, allowing all the legs to project 12 inches below the bottom face. Turn it right side up on its legs and nail the top on, having its rear edge even with the outside face of the rear legs, allowing it to project at the ends and in front ½ inch over the outside face of the legs. Remove the covers from two of the remaining boxes. Stand one box on its end and set another box upon it endwise, then nail together and put in the shelves at the height desired. Do the same with the other two boxes and set each pair in its place on the top, having their backs even with the lower portion of the stand. Put the facing strips on the end of the lower portion and also on the ends and over the front edge of each of the upper portions, having their outer edges even with the outside edge of the closets. Fit and hang the doors and screw on the pull-knobs and buttons. Screw two hooks in the under-side edge of the top of the packing-box, and cut and lay a broom handle in them, upon which may be arranged a sliding curtain. Cut two broom handles to fit between the upper closets, and place them about as shown, and fasten them with a nail driven through the side of the closet box into their ends—the lower one to carry a splasher and the upper one for towels. A mirror may also be fitted as shown. Put on the upper top, keeping its rear edge even with the outer face of the rear legs, allowing it to project ½ inch over the outer face of the legs at the ends and ½ inch over the facing strips in front.

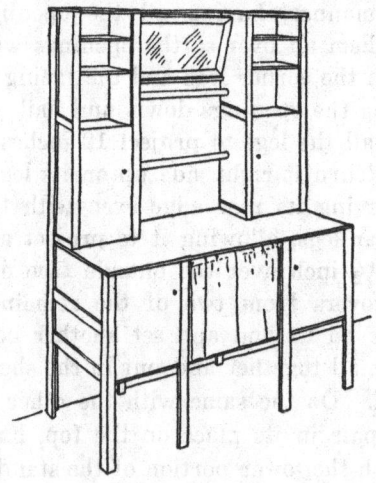

CHILD'S WASHSTAND AND DRESSER
Illustration 95   *Figure 1*

A similar style of Dresser as shown in Illustration 94, but a smaller type suitable for a child, being made with smaller boxes and shorter legs.

The upper closed compartment and one towel rack are dispensed with.

Requirements:

Cupboards. 4 Canned-soup Boxes (about 8¼ in. deep, 11¼ in. wide, 17¼ in. long).

Middle Compartment. 1 Small Packing-box (about 16½ in. square, 16½ in. long).

Upper Compartments. 2 Borax-soap Boxes (about 6 in. deep, 10⅞ in. wide, 18¾ in. long).

Lower Top. 1 Piece ½ in. thick, 1½ in. wider than the length of the cupboard boxes, by 2 in. longer than the packing-box and twice the width of the cupboard box combined.

Upper Top. 1 Piece ½ in. thick, 1 in. wider than the outside depth of the box, 2 in. longer than the packing-box and twice the width of the cupboard box combined.

Doors. 2 Pieces ⅜ in. thick, 2¼ in. narrower than the outside width of the cupboard box, and the length equal to twice the outside depth of the cupboard box.

Facing Strips. 4 Strips ⅜ in. thick, 1¼ in. wide, and the length equal to the outside length of the upper compartment box. 4 Strips ⅜ in. thick, 1¾ in. wide, 6½ in. longer than twice the outside depth of the cupboard boxes. 4 Strips ⅜ in. thick, 1¾ in. wide, and the length 2¾ in. shorter than the cupboard boxes.

Legs. 2 Strips ⅜ in. thick, 1⅜ in. wide, 6½ in. longer than twice the outside depth of the cupboard boxes. 2 Strips ⅜ in. thick, 1¾ in. wide, 6½ in. longer than twice the outside depth of the cupboard boxes. 2 Strips ⅜ in. thick, 1⅜ in. wide, 6½ in. longer than the outside length of the upper compartment box and twice the outside depth of the cupboard boxes combined. 2 Strips ⅜ in. thick, 1¾ in. wide, 6½ in. longer than the outside length of the upper compartment box and twice the outside depth of the soup boxes combined.

Rods. 2 Broom Handles.

Hardware. 2 brass buttons. 4 hinges, 1¼ in. (butts). 2 pull-knobs.

Mirror. 1 Mirror.

Construction:

Make the legs, two 6½ inches longer than twice the outside depth of the cupboard boxes, and two 6½ inches longer than twice the outside depth of the cupboard boxes and the outside length of the upper compartment box combined. Remove the ends from the four cupboard boxes and the cover from the packing-box. Lay a cupboard box on its side and place another on its side upon it, and nail together through the abutting sides. Do the same with the other two cupboard boxes. Make the packing-box the same width as the depth of a pair of cupboard boxes, then place the packing-box on its end and set a pair of the cupboard boxes on their sides upon it. Match their edges and nail together. Join the other pair to the other end of the packing-box in the same manner, having all the openings facing alike. Turn them all over so the openings will all face up, and put on the corner and the facing strip legs, having the edge of the facing strips even with the inside edge of the middle compartment. Reverse, having the openings down, and nail on the rear legs, allowing all the legs to project $6\frac{1}{2}$ inches below the bottom face. Turn it right side up, on its legs, and nail the top on, having its rear edge even with the outside face of the rear legs, allowing it to project at the ends and in front $\frac{1}{2}$ inch over the outside face of the legs. Remove the covers from the remaining boxes and put in the shelves at the heights desired. Set each box in its place on the top, having their backs even with the lower portion of the stand.

Put the facing strips on the end of the lower portion and also over the front edge of each of the upper portions, having their outer edges even with the outside edge of the box. Fit and hang the doors and screw on the pull-knobs and buttons. Screw two hooks in the under-side edge of the top of the packing-box, and cut and lay a broom handle in them upon which may be arranged a sliding curtain. Cut a broom handle to fit between the upper boxes and place it about as shown, to serve as a towel rack. A mirror may also be fitted as shown. Put on the upper top, keeping its rear edge even with the outer face of the rear legs, allowing it to project $\frac{1}{2}$ inch over the outer face of the legs at the ends and $\frac{1}{2}$ inch over the facing strips in front.

CHINA CLOSET

Illustration 96   *Figure 1*

This is composed of two side closets, each fitted with shelves and glazed doors hinged upon the outer face, there being three lights to each door. Between the closets is a recessed section, the lower portion of which is a cupboard with an open compartment directly above for water-pitcher, the recess above being fitted with cup-and-saucer shelves.

The cupboard is fitted with shelves for containing small table linen.

Requirements:

Body. 3 Carpet-sweeper Boxes (about 11¾ in. deep, 15½ in. wide, 55½ in. long).

Shelves. 19 Pieces ½ in. thick, the width equal to the inside depth of the box, and the length equal to the inside width of the box. 2 Pieces ½ in. thick, 2½ in. wide, and the length equal to the inside width of the box.

Top. 2 Pieces ½ in. thick, 3 in. wider than the outside depth of the box, and 3 in. longer than the outside width of the box with the thickness of the side of the box added.

Corner Legs. 4 Strips ½ in. thick, 1½ in. wide, 6 in. longer than the outside length of the box. 4 Strips ½ in. thick, 2 in. wide, 6 in. longer than the outside length of the box.

Facing Strip Legs. 4 Strips ½ in. thick, 2 in. wide, 6 in. longer than the outside length of the box.

Facing Strips. 4 Strips ½ in. thick, 2 in. wide, 2½ in. shorter than the outside width of the box. 2 Strips ½ in. thick, 2 in. wide, 2 in. shorter than the outside width of the box. 4 Strips ½ in. thick, 2 in. wide, 3 in. shorter than the outside depth of the box. 1 Strip ½ in. thick, 2 in. wide, 3 in. shorter than the inside width of the box. 1 Strip ½ in. thick, 2 in. wide, 20½ in. long. (Vertical strip between the cupboard doors.)

Cupboard Doors. 2 Pieces ½ in. thick, 2 in. narrower than one half the outside width of the box, by 20½ in. long.

Sash Door Frames. 4 Strips ½ in. thick, 2 in. wide, 1 in. longer than the outside length of the box. 4 Strips ½ in. thick, 2 in. wide, 2½ in. shorter than the outside width of the box. 4 Strips ½ in. thick, 1¼ in. wide, 2½ in. shorter than the outside width of the box.

Glass Lights for Doors. 6 Window-glass Lights, 2 in. narrower than the inside width of the box, by 2 in. less than one third the outside length of the box.

Hardware. 4 1¾ in. brass hinges (butts) with screws. 4 small brass knobs. 2 brass buttons for cupboard doors. 6 2 in. brass hinges (butts) and screws. 2 brass pull-knobs. 2 brass hooks, screws, and screw-eyes for large doors.

Construction:

Make the legs 6 inches longer than the outside length of the box. Remove the covers. Fit and nail seven shelves each in two of the boxes. Space the shelves to suit the various pieces of china they are to contain. Or, if made as shown in the illustration, the height of the respective compartments, naming the bottom one first, then each consecutively to the top, would be as follows: 8 inches, 8 inches, 6 inches, 5 inches, 5 inches, 6 inches, 6 inches, 7 inches. Drive the nails from the outside, through the sides and bottom of the box, into the edges of the shelves, using $1\frac{1}{2}$ inch wire brads spaced not more than 2 inches apart. Remove one end from the third box and set it in, having its outer face 22 inches from the other end to form a cupboard compartment, and nail it. Fit and nail three shelves evenly spaced in this compartment. Fit and nail a shelf 11 inches from the end which has been set in, to form the compartment above the cupboard. Eight and a half inches from this shelf nail one of the $2\frac{1}{2}$-inch-wide shelves, and the other one 7 inches from this last one. Place one of the end closets on its side upon the floor and set the middle section on its side upon it, having both open compartments facing the same way, the cupboard compartment being directly over the largest compartment of the end section or closet. Match their edges and nail securely together. Join the other end section to the middle one in a similar manner. Nail on the corner and facing strip legs (there being two of the latter) on both front and rear. Have them project evenly over each compartment. Stand the closet right end up on its legs and set the tops in place and nail them, allowing them to project $1\frac{1}{2}$ inches over the outside face of the closets all around. Fit the top facing strip on the back of the middle section between the tops of the end sections. It should project $1\frac{1}{2}$ inches into the recess of the middle section. Put on the front facing strips between the corner and facing strip legs at both the top and bottom of the closets. The upper edge of the top ones bears against the under side of the top, while the top edge of the lower ones is even with the inside face of the bottom of the closets. The lower facing strips across the ends and in front are all to be at the same level and in line. The top edge of the facing strip over the cupboard doors will be level with the upper face of the shelf. Nail the ends of the vertical cupboard strip to horizontal strips above and below it. Fit and hang the cupboard doors and screw on the pull-knobs and buttons.

Make the inside width of the sash door frame the same as the width between the corner leg and the facing strip leg, and the inside length the same as the distance between the facing strips at the top and bottom of the closet. Halve the ends of the frame strips and glue or nail together, and cut the rabbet for the glass as described for Picture Frame No. 1, Illustration 72. The 1¼-inch-wide strips should be rabbeted. Place two across each door at points to make three equal panels. Fit and hang the doors, put in the glass lights, and screw on the pull-knobs, hooks, and screw-eyes.

276 BOX FURNITURE

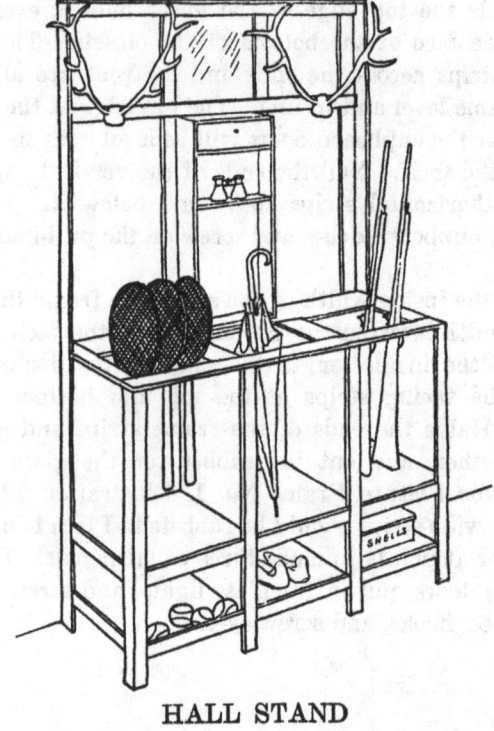

HALL STAND

Illustration 97 *Figures 1 and 2*

The stand provides space for tennis rackets and balls, umbrellas and overshoes, guns and ammunition. There is a drawer for gloves, a shelf for spy-glasses and clothes-brush, and hangers for hats and coats. The lower row of boxes has open ends facing front, while the three boxes above them have one open end and one open side each. The portion above these is mere framework without any back. In the center is held the seventh box, standing on end with its cover removed, containing shelves and a drawer (the eighth box). The middle space above the drawer contains a mirror.

Requirements:

Body. 3 Condensed-milk Boxes (about 7¼ in. deep, 13 in. wide, 19¾ in. long). 3 Butter Boxes (12½ in. deep, 13 in. wide, 26 in. long). 1 Raisin Box (about 3½ in. deep, 10½ in. wide, 18 in. long).

Drawer. 1 Cigar Box (2½ in. deep, 3¼ in. wide, 9¾ in. long).

Legs. 2 Strips ½ in. thick, 2 in. wide, 5 ft. 10 in. long. 2 Strips ½ in. thick, 2½ in. wide, 5 ft. 10 in. long. 2 Strips ½ in. thick, 2 in. wide, about 37 in. long. 2 Strips ½ in. thick, 2½ in. wide, about 37 in. long.

Facing Strips. 2 Strips ½ in. thick, 2½ in. wide, about 37 in. long.

Intermediate Legs. 2 Strips ½ in. thick, 2½ in. wide, 5 ft. 10 in. long.

Sundry Facing Strips. 14 Strips ½ in. thick, 2½ in. wide, about 15 in. long.

Crosspieces. 1 Strip ½ in. thick, 2½ in. wide, 40 in. long. 2 Strips ½ in. thick, 2½ in. wide, 39 in. long.

Hooks. 2 Pairs Antlers (or their equivalent).

Mirror. 1 Mirror.

Construction:

Make the legs, two 5 feet and 10 inches long, and two 4 inches longer than the combined outside length of the butter box and depth of the milk box. Make a pencil line completely around one of the milk boxes 12 inches from one end, and cut the box in two, sawing on the line. Do the same with two others. There are now three boxes 12 inches long, each open at one end. Place one of these boxes on its side, and upon it place another likewise, the open ends facing the same way. Join them together by nailing through the abutting sides. Place the third box in the same way upon the second one and nail it in the same manner. Match all their edges before nailing. Remove the covers and one end from each of the three butter boxes, and place and join them together the same as those for the lower compartments. Clinch the points of the nails which join them so that they may be firmly held together. Place the lower set of boxes on the work bench, flat side down, and stand the upper set on their ends upon them, having the open compartments facing the same way as shown in the illustration. Match the edges of both sets and join them together. Turn both sets over, all open sides of the compartments facing up, and put on the short legs, also the two short facing strip legs which go between them, having their upper ends even with the top edge of the upper compartments, the edges of the strips projecting equally on each side, and all the legs projecting 4 inches below the bottom face of the stand. Reverse the stand and nail on the long corner legs and long facing strips which extend between them and to the same height. Set the stand right end up on its legs and nail one of the shorter crosspieces on, placing its edge up on the inner face of the rear corner legs, and nail it to them and to the long facing strips, keeping its upper edge 12 inches below the top of the legs. Put the other crosspiece of the same length on in the same manner, having its upper edge even with the top of the legs. Nail the last and longer crosspiece to the top of the legs and to the edge of the last crosspiece put on, having its rear edge even with the rear face of the legs. Fit and nail two rows of facing strips across the front of the lower compartments, having the bottom edge of the lower ones even with the bottom face of the stand, and the bottom edge of the upper ones even with the inside top face of the lower compartments. Put a facing strip on the top of the front legs, having its ends and outer edge even with the outer face of the legs. Put a facing strip across each end from the front one to the inner face of the rear leg, cutting it out to allow one side of the rear leg to set in so that the outside edge of the strip will be even with the outer face of the leg. Put one between the last two along the back, having its back edge even with the inner face of the rear legs, and put the two short ones on the partitions dividing the three upper compartments, each edge having an equal projection. Remove the cover of the raisin box and fit it between the rear facing strips, cutting it down in width and length, if necessary. Nail it in place, keeping its rear face even with the rear face of the ex-tended facing strips. Fit and nail the shelves in place and re-move the cover from the cigar box. Put the cigar box in place and screw the small brass knob at the center of its front face. Fas-ten the antlers on the lower crosspiece and place the mir-ror in the mid-dle space be-tween the cross-pieces, and se-cure it in place with glazier's points or large-headed tacks. The other two small and two large spaces in the high frame are left open.

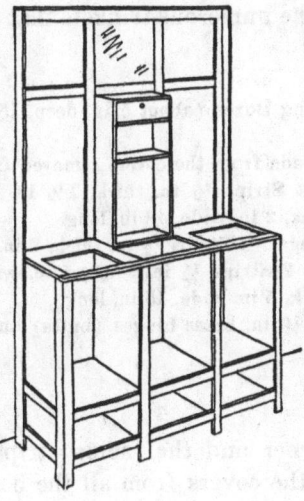

BOX FURNITURE

BOY'S DELIGHT

Illustration 98   *Figure 1*

An adaptation of the "Silverette" and a portion of the Umbrella- and Overshoe-Stand combined, and is designed to hold the numerous trinkets that delight the boy.

Requirements:

Body. 8 Herring Boxes (about 5 in. deep, 15 in. wide, 15½ in. long).

Cover Lids. Made from the covers removed from the boxes.

Corner Legs. 4 Strips ½ in. thick, 1½ in. wide, 48 in. long. 4 Strips ½ in. thick, 2 in. wide, 48 in. long.

Facing Strip Legs. 4 Strips ½ in. thick, 2 in. wide, 48 in. long.

Facing Strips. 2 Strips ½ in. thick, 5 in. wide, 14½ in. long. 4 Strips ½ in. thick, 5 in. wide, 15 in. long.

Hardware. 4 1½ in. brass hinges (butts) and screws. 2 pull-knobs.

Construction:

Make the corner and the facing strip legs 48 inches long. Remove the covers from all the boxes. Place one of the boxes on its side on the floor, and upon it set another box on its side, with both open compartments facing the same way. Match their edges and join them by nailing the abutting sides together. Upon this second box place a third one on its side and join them in a similar manner, being careful that when joined they are in a straight line. With three more boxes, make another set in the same manner. Place both sets on their sides, spaced 6 inches apart, the open top of one set facing the closed bottoms of the other set, and nail a corner leg on at each end, allowing the legs to project 4 inches over the bottom face of one set. Use the try-square as a guide to have the legs at right angles with the top edge of the set of boxes. Reverse them and nail the corner legs on the opposite corners and set the piece upon its legs. Nail on the four facing strip legs, having the center of the strip directly over the box joints. Place and nail the two remaining boxes between the facing strip legs, setting the upper edge of one the thickness of the cover below the top of the strips, and the bottom of the other 6 inches above the top edge of the upper set of three. These two upper boxes in the middle section will have covers made in two parts hinged together, the rear part 4 inches wide, to be nailed on the rear top part of the box, with its back edge even with the rear outside face of the box. Hang the wide portion of the cover to this narrow portion with the butts or hinges, and screw on the lifting knob. Put the wide facing strips on the inside face of the legs between the corner legs and the top box, both front and rear, and between the corner legs at each end. The upper boxes in the middle section may have partitions placed in them as desired.

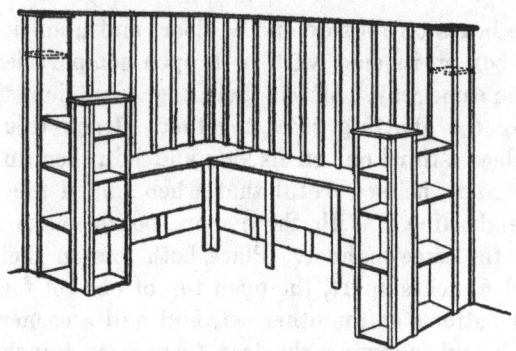

CLUB-ROOM CORNER SEAT

Illustration 99 *Figure 1*

A unique Corner Seat made by the author for the club-room at Copenhagen Settlement, Denmark, in the fall of 1907. A recent letter states that the seat has been in constant use and is as strong as when built. It consists of two packing-boxes on legs, the rear edge of which supports a paneled back upheld at each end by a pedestal. A double-section library, filled with the club books, flanks both ends of the seat, the pedestals giving a substantial end finish to the back.

The paneled back is a protection to the wall, and upon its face were hung three flat-back cushions, about 5 inches thick, filled with the shavings. Each shelf in the pedestals holds a jar of water from which trail growing ivy vines. The practical and artistic effect of such a combination may readily be imagined.

The seat covers are loose and removable, giving easy access to the compartments beneath them, which afford large stowaway facilities.

BOX FURNITURE

Being portable, this seat may easily be moved to another corner if necessary.

Requirements:

Seats. 1 Packing-box (9½ in. deep, 21 in. wide, 40 in. long). 1 Packing-box (9½ in. deep, 21 in. wide, 49 in. long).

Vine Pedestal. 2 Special Boxes (7½ in. square, 47 in. long, and, being an odd size, will probably have to be made from the material of other boxes).

Oblong Bookcases. 6 Small Butter Boxes (8 in. deep, 10 in. wide, 15 in. long).

Square Bookcases. 2 Silk Boxes (7½ in. deep, 7½ in. wide, 35 in. long).

Seat Covers. 1 Piece ¾ in. thick, 21½ in. wide, 40 in. long. 1 Piece ¾ in. thick, 21½ in. wide, 49 in. long.

Square Bookcase Shelves. 6 Pieces ½ in. thick, the width and depth of the inside of the box.

Vine Pedestal Shelves. 2 Pieces ½ in. thick, the width and depth of the inside of the box.

False Top. 4 Pieces ½ in. thick, 2 in. larger each way than the end of the pedestal boxes.

Corner Legs. 2 Strips ⅝ in. thick, 1½ in. wide, 18¼ in. long. 2 Strips ⅝ in. thick, 2 in. wide, 18¼ in. long.

Facing Strip Legs. 10 Strips ⅝ in. thick, 2 in. wide, 18¼ in. long.

Vine Pedestal Corner Trim. 4 Strips ⅜ in. thick, ⅞ in. wide, the length equal to the inside length of the box. 4 Strips ⅜ in. thick, 1¼ in. wide, the length equal to the inside length of the box.

Vine Pedestal Facing Strips. 4 Strips ⅜ in. thick, 1¼ in. wide, the length equal to the outside length of the box.

Square Bookcase Corner Trim. 4 Strips ⅜ in. thick, ⅞ in. wide, the length equal to the outside length of the box. 4 Strips ⅜ in. thick, 1¼ in. wide, the length equal to the outside length of the box.

Square Bookcase Facing Strips. 4 Strips ⅝ in. thick, ⅞ in. wide, the length equal to the outside length of the box.

Seat Cleats. 5 Strips ⅝ in. thick, 2½ in. wide, 18½ in. long.

Paneled Back. 22 Strips ¼ in. thick, 5 in. wide, about 29¼ in. long. 24 Strips ¼ in. thick, 1 in. wide, about 26¼ in. long.

Top of the Back. 1 Strip ½ in. thick, 2 in. wide, 42 in. long. 1 Strip ½ in. thick, 2 in. wide, 72 in. long.

Construction:

Make two corner and ten facing strip legs for the seat —one corner leg and six facing strip legs 17¼ inches long, and the others 18¼ inches long. The short legs are for the rear of the seat, and when nailed in place their upper ends are to be 1 inch below the top edge of the seat boxes. The sheathing of the paneled back will project 1 inch below the top of the seat boxes and will nail to them in the rear, while the lower end of the 1-inch-wide joint strips will be even with the top of the cover to allow the cover to fit under them and against the sheathing forming the back.

Remove the covers from all of the boxes except the vine pedestal boxes. Turn the shorter seat box on its side and nail the short corner leg, 1, on the corner which is to fit in the corner of the room. On the same end of the box, but at the other corner, put a short facing strip leg, 1, allowing it to project one half its width over the side. When the seat boxes are placed together, the center of this leg will cover the joint. Nail the long leg, 2, and the short leg, 3, at the other end, having their outer edges even with the end of the box. Put No. 4 (short) leg half-way between No. 3 and the corner leg, having all their upper ends 1 inch below the top of the box, except No. 2, which will be even with the top. Turn the box on its side, that side with the three legs being on the floor. Nail the long leg, 5, and the short leg, 6, on the longer seat box, and place its opposite end upon the upper side of the shorter seat box, having its side against the overlapping leg on the end of the shorter seat box. Match their edges and nail them together, putting corner leg, 2, the reverse way in the angle formed by the junction of the boxes. Turn the boxes over upon the legs and nail on short legs 7 and 9 and long legs 8 and 10, having them evenly spaced front and rear between the legs at the end.

Make the seat covers for each box 1½ inches wider than the outside width of the box and of the same length as the outside length of the box. They may be made with either two or three widths of board, with cleats placed on the under side about 4 inches from the end, and one in the center of the long seat, having each end of the cleats 1½ inches from the side edges of the cover. It will be necessary to cut ½ inch off the front edge of the shorter cover the width of the longer cover, as shown in Fig. 2. Allow the front edges of the seats to be even with the front face of the legs. The vine pedestal may be without ends, made of four pieces of equal width and

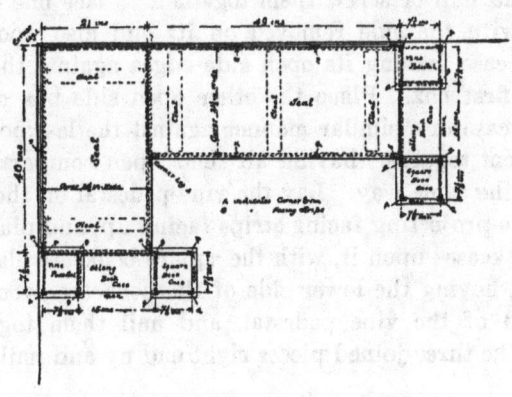

length, formed as described for the Cast Pedestal, Illustration 3. Fit and nail the shelf inside of each vine pedestal box 8 inches (or at a suitable depth to suit the flower-pot it will contain) from one end, which will be the top end. Nail the corner trim A on two corners and the facing strips B on the sides near the opposite corners, as shown in Fig. 2, having the facing strips overlapping or projecting one half their width over the corners of the box. Fit and nail the shelves in the square bookcase boxes, spacing them to suit the books they will contain; or, if preferable, made like the illustration, the heights of the compartments, named from the bottom up, would be about 10 inches, 8 inches, 7 inches, and 7 inches. Put on the corner trim and facing strips the same as described above for the vine pedestal.

Remove one side from each of two of the oblong bookcase boxes. Turn the square bookcase open side down on the floor and place one of the remaining boxes on its end upon it between the projecting facing strips, having one side of the box even with one end of the square bookcase, and nail or screw them together. Place one of the boxes with the side removed on its end also upon the square case, having its open side edges against the side of the first box. Place the other open side box on the square case in a similar manner against the last box and nail them together, having all their open compartments facing the same way. Lay the vine pedestal on the floor with the projecting facing strips facing up, and place the two bookcases upon it, with the square bookcase also facing up, having the lower side of the bookcase even with the end of the vine pedestal, and nail them together. Stand the three joined pieces right end up and nail a top on the square bookcase and also the vine pedestal, allowing it to project 1 inch over on all sides. The tops for the vine pedestals must have a suitable opening cut in them to admit the flower-pot which the shelf supports. The openings may be easily cut after the tops are nailed on.

Construct the other oblong bookcase from the remaining boxes and join the other square bookcase and pedestal to it in the same manner. The open side of the oblong bookcase will face to the left in one, while in the other it will face to the right, as you face the open side of the square bookcase. Place one section against each end of the corner seat and nail or screw them firmly together.

Select a strip having a straight edge and not less than 6 feet long. Lay it on the floor and tack it with nails driven two thirds down. Lay one of the 5-inch-wide sheathing strips which form the back also on the floor, at right angles to and near the end of the first strip, and tack it also. Place another sheathing strip against this, and over the joint formed by their abutting sides nail a 1-inch-wide joint strip, and continue to lay the sheathing, placing and nailing a joint strip over each joint, until 14 sheathing strips are thus joined together, having the end of each joint and sheathing strip against the first strip tacked to the floor. Use nails not more than $\frac{1}{8}$ inch longer than the thickness of both strips, otherwise the back will be nailed to the floor and cannot easily be released. This forms the long side of the back. Remove it, and with the remaining strips make the other side in a similar manner. Place them in position, at the back of the seat boxes, with the lower edge of the sheathing resting on the top of the legs and the lower end of the joint strips on top of the cover, one end being against the corner trim of the vine pedestal and the other end even with the outside corner face of the box, and screw it through the sheathing into the seat boxes. Put on the other portion of the back in a similar way, joining their ends to the corner trim of the vine pedestals with joint strips nailed to each, and their ends in the corner nailed through the side of one into the edge of the other and joined with the joint strips also. Fit and nail the 2-inch-wide top strip placed on its flat side on the top of each side, allowing it to project 1 inch over the face of the joint strips. The seat, now being complete, may be moved bodily into the corner awaiting it.

BOX FURNITURE 289

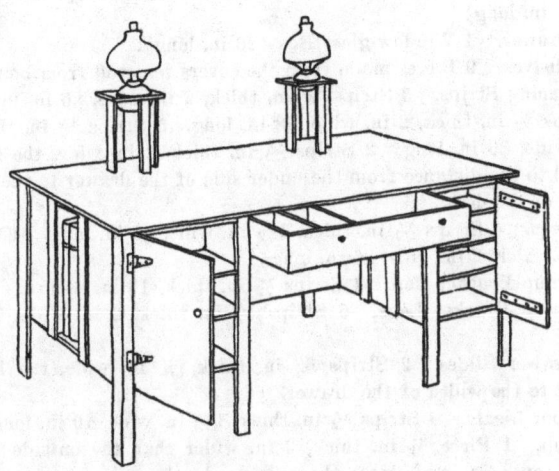

COMBINATION DESK, READING-TABLE
AND BOOKCASE

Illustration 100 *Figures 1 and 2*

This article of furniture was made by the author to meet the requirements of the winter manager of a coal-mine located in the arctic region. He said: "Our space is very limited. We need something to serve as a writing-desk, with ample stationery closets, book-shelves for our library, magazines, and newspapers, that can be used as a reading-table and support a light which our cat, who has a fondness for lamps, cannot overturn during our three months' period of total darkness."

This is much simpler to make than one would imagine, so study it carefully.

Requirements:

Body. 8 Condensed-milk Boxes (about 7¼ in. deep, 13 in. wide, 19¾ in. long).

Drawer. 1 Window-glass Box (26 in. long).

Shelves. 9 Pieces made from the covers removed from boxes.

Facing Strips. 3 Strips ½ in. thick, 2 in. wide, 26 in. long. 2 Strips ½ in. thick, 2 in. wide, 38 in. long. 5 Strips ½ in. thick, 2 in. wide, 20 in. long. 2 Strips ½ in. thick, 2 in. wide, the length equal to the distance from the under side of the drawer to the lower edge of the desk.

Legs. 4 Strips ½ in. thick, 1½ in. wide, 26 in. long. 4 Strips ½ in. thick, 2 in. wide, 26 in. long.

Lamp Bracket Top. 4 Strips ½ in. thick, 10 in. square.

Lamp Bracket Legs. 6 Strips ½ in. thick, 2 in. wide, 12 in. long.

Drawer Slides. 2 Strips ⅜ in. thick, ¾ in. wide, the length equal to the width of the drawer.

Door Cleats. 4 Strips ½ in. thick, 1½ in. wide, 10 in. long.

Top. 1 Piece ¾ in. thick, 3 in. wider than the outside depth with cover on, and twice the outside depth with cover removed, and 3 in. longer than four times the outside width of the box.

Hardware. 4 tee hinges. 4 pull-knobs.

Construction:

Make the six corner legs 26 inches long. Remove the covers carefully from six of the boxes and one side from each of the other two. In four of the boxes, 10 inches from one end, fit a shelf the full depth of the box and fasten the shelves in with 1½ inch brads, driven through the sides and bottom of the box into the edges of the shelves. These four boxes form the library portion, as shown by Fig. 2. Take one of the four and turn it on its side, then place another sidewise upon the first, match their edges, and nail the boxes together by driving through their sides. Place another box on its side upon the second one, then the fourth box upon the third, joining them all as the first two, taking care that all open sides face alike and that like compartments are kept in line. Lay all four boxes down as one, upon their bottoms. Nail a corner leg at the open side corner of each end box, keeping the upper end of the leg even with that end of the boxes which has the smaller compartment. Turn them all upside down and they will all stand bottom up. On each end box place upon its flat side one of the boxes from which you removed the side, so that the remaining closed sides will face each other. Match them to the boxes upon which they rest, and get all the edges even and nail them to the end boxes. Upon the boxes last added, place the other two boxes, one upon each, open side up, and nail them to the others. There is now a pile of boxes three high at each end, lying flat sides down. While they lie in this position, fit the shelves in the two top boxes just added, spacing them to suit the material they are to contain. Fasten the shelves with $1\frac{1}{2}$ inch brads driven through the sides of the boxes into the edges of the shelves. Put on the corner legs, one on each outer corner, and nail a facing strip, or intermediate leg, on each opposite corner, having the inner edge of the facing strips even with the outside face of the box. Between these facing strips will be fitted the drawer. Fit the doors in place between the legs and facing strips just added, then put the cleats on the doors near the top and bottom, placed so they will clear the shelves when the doors close. Put the hinges on, keeping the middle of the hinge about 4 inches from each end of the door. Hang the doors so they will open one right and the other left hand. Screw the knobs on the doors 6 inches down from the top of the door and 2 inches from the edge. Turn the whole piece over and stand it upon its legs. Nail on the three facing strips which cover the joints of the boxes and also act as intermediate legs, two of which form part of the lamp bracket. Remove one side from the window-glass box, and, if the box is not the proper length to fit in the recess, set the end in and shorten it and fit it in place. Nail the slides on the body at both sides of recess directly under the ends of the drawer, keeping the upper edge of the drawer even with the top of the facing strips. Push the drawer in until its front face is even with the face of the facing strips. Nail a small block behind it on each side for a stop. Place such partitions in the drawer as you may wish, and screw on the knobs 4 inches from each end and at the center vertically. Nail on the seven remaining facing strips which cover the box joints only, two at each outer end and three in the recess. The two end ones in the recess will extend from the under side of the drawer slide to the lower edge of the body. Put on the top, allowing the edges to project 1 inch over the outside face of the legs all around. Cut the edge of the top on the library side $1\frac{1}{2}$ inches deep and 2 inches wide to admit the two facing strips which form a part of the lamp support, and nail the cover on. Fit and nail two pieces 2 inches long, 1 inch wide, and $\frac{3}{4}$ inch thick to fit the cut outside the lamp bracket facing strips. Place two of the 10-inch-square lamp bracket tops on the bench, flat sides down, with the grain of the wood of one at right angles with the other, and glue and clamp them together, holding them tightly for twenty-four hours. Measure the lamp and cut a hole with the keyhole-saw the proper diameter to suit the lamp, the center of the hole being in the center of the top. Smooth the edges of the hole with sandpaper and cut the bracket legs so they stand above the main top exactly the same distance as does the facing strip. Place the bracket top upon the facing strip, keeping the edge even with the outer face of the strip and projecting equally on each side, and nail it with two long brads to the top end of the strip. Place a leg under the opposite side and set and nail it in the same way. Do the same with the other two legs. While keeping all the legs perfectly straight or plumb, nail them at the bottom ends. Use an awl to start the holes and toe the brads in, using 1¼ inch brads. Repeat this for the other lamp bracket. Doors may be hung for the end compartments if preferred.

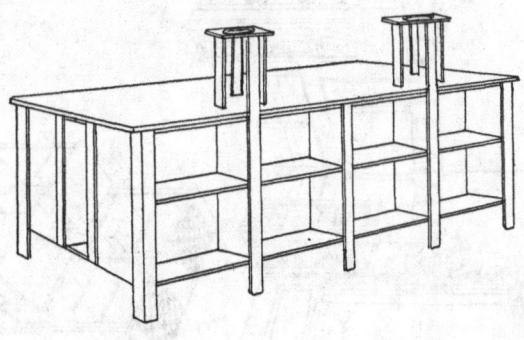

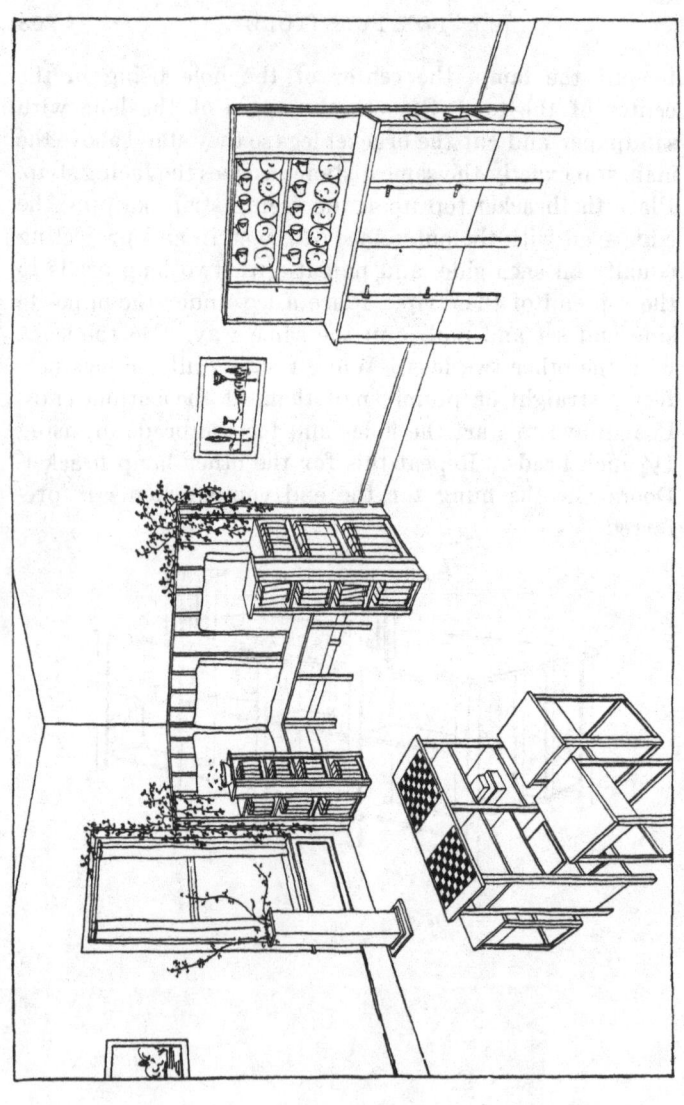

A Corner of the Copenhagen Club-room

GAME-TABLE   CLUB-ROOM STOOLS
CLUB-ROOM CORNER SEAT
BRANCH PEDESTAL   COPENHAGEN SIDEBOARD

Color Scheme:
  Flemish oak.
  Yellow.

Woodwork:
  Flemish oak (paint).

Furniture:
  Flemish oak (stain).

Walls:
  Yellow.

Ceiling:
  Yellow of a lighter shade.

Corner-seat Pillows:
  Olive-green burlap.

China:
  White, with green and yellow design.

Floor:
  Flemish oak (stained).

Plants:
  Vines, growing plants, and cut flowers with yellow blossoms.

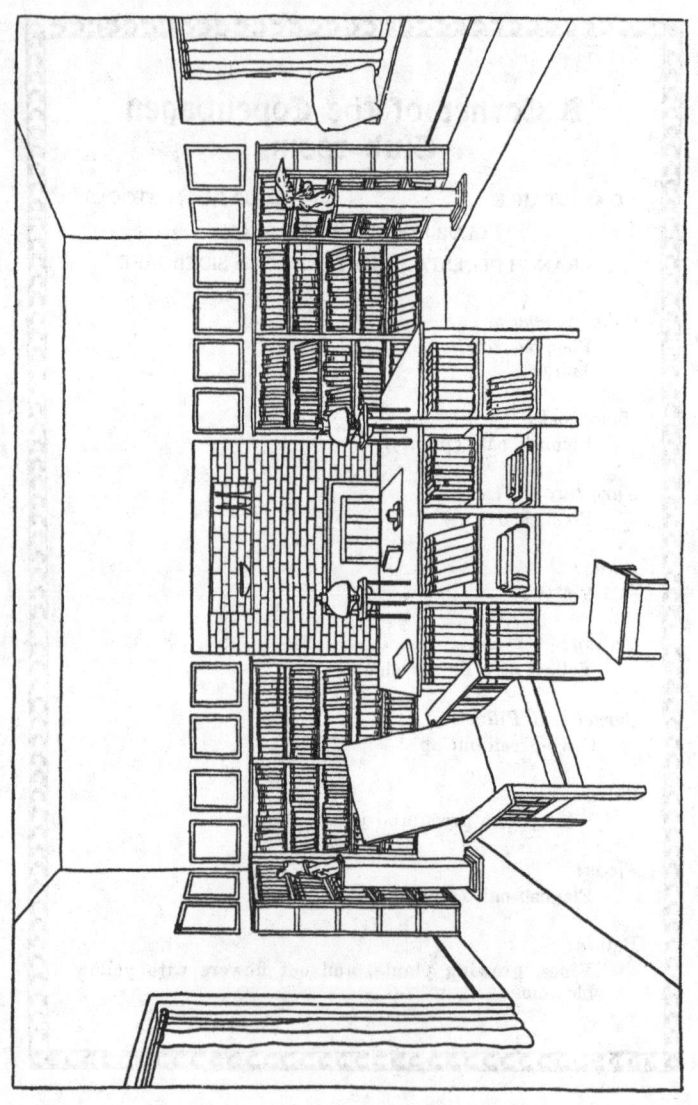

Library or Study

TWO SMALL 500-VOLUME BOOKCASES

CAST PEDESTAL   FOOTSTOOL

COMBINATION DESK,
READING-TABLE AND BOOKCASE

Color Scheme:
  Black.
  Moss green.

Woodwork:
  Black paint.

Furniture:
  Black paint.

Walls:
  Moss green.

Ceiling:
  Green, in lighter tone than the walls.

Hangings and Pillows:
  Plain green burlap or canvas, or with motif appliquéd in black and gold.

Curtains:
  Cream-colored muslin.

Floor:
  Black paint, with large green rug.

Plants:
  Growing palms, and plants with either red, yellow, or white blossoms.

The First Process in the Construction of the Allendale Sideboard

The Tool-chest, given to the Author by One Hundred Friends

The Rough Material Arrives

The Spitzbergen Sideboard and Hall Stand

Combination Desk, Reading-table, and Bookcase
Rear View

The Game-table in the Club-room of the Copenhagen Settlement

The China-closet

The Copenhagen Sideboard, 'Closed and Opened

The "Dresserette," Opened

The Upright Clock

The Greek-cross Tea-table, Opened

Washstand and Dresser

The Greek-cross Tea-table Closed

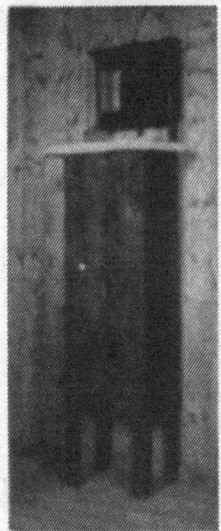
The "Shavingette," Closed

The Office Washstand, Opened

Copenhagen Corner Seat, in the Club-room of the Copenhagen Settlement

www.ingramcontent.com/pod-product-compliance
Lightning Source LLC
Chambersburg PA
CBHW010929180426
43194CB00045B/2836